ENERGY IN ISLAM

A Scientific Approach to Preserving Our Health and the Environment

Tallal Alie Turfe

Published by
Tahrike Tarsile Qur'an, Inc.

Publishers and Distributors of Holy Qur'an
80-08 51ˢᵗ Avenue
Elmhurst, New York 11373-4141
www.koranusa.org
E-mail: orders@koranusa.org

First U.S. Edition 2010

ISBN: 978-1-879402-31-7
Library of Congress Control Number: 2010938389

TABLE OF CONTENTS

PREFACE   1

ACKNOWLEDGMENTS   3

ABOUT THE AUTHOR   5

POEM: ENERGY   9

INTRODUCTION   11

CHAPTER 1: CONCEPT OF ENERGY   15

CHAPTER 2: FORMS OF ENERGY   31

CHAPTER 3: APPLICATION OF ENERGY FORMS IN ISLAM   41

CHAPTER 4: ENERGY TRANSFORMATION   57

CHAPTER 5: ENERGY: ENVIRONMENTALISM AND SOVEREIGNTY AS
STEWARDSHIP   73

CHAPTER 6: ENERGIZING THE ISLAMIC PERSONALITY   83

CHAPTER 7: SELECTED EXAMPLES OF ENERGY IN THE QUR'AN   99

CHAPTER 8: PHILOSOPHY OF ENERGY IN ISLAM   107

CHAPTER 9: MANIFESTATION OF ENERGY: PROPHET MOHAMMAD
AND IMAM ALI IBN ABI TALIB   125

CHAPTER 10: ENERGY CASE EXAMPLES: HEROES OF ISLAM   139

CHAPTER 11: ENERGY AND SCIENCE: CONTRIBUTIONS OF
IMAM JA'FAR AS-SADIQ   155

EPILOGUE   159

BIBLIOGRAPHY   161

FOOTNOTES   169

PREFACE

This book is written to explore the concept of energy and how it affects the Universe, the Earth, and our daily lives. Aside from the spiritual aspect, not too much has been written on the subject of energy as it relates to Islam. It is hoped that Islamic scholars will use this book as a benchmark to further research and explore the importance of energy.

Each of us goes through life wanting to understand more about God's Creation and how we live and function within it. Knowledge affords us the opportunity to have a deeper sense of appreciation for the marvels of existence and how we can equip ourselves to be better Muslims. As we strive towards self-actualization, we find ourselves thirsty and eager to learn even more about Islam. This book will enlighten those who wish to reflect on Islam, with particular focus on a fascinating and illuminating concept – energy!

We live and take life for granted. We function from day to day not reflecting on what is our purpose in life. How many of us have tested ourselves to see that we are in conformity with God's Commands? After all, our life is but a test for a higher reward or eternal damnation. Our faith and good deeds flanked by the search for truth and demonstration of patience are the criteria that enable us to successfully pass the test. But what is the test? It is God's Decree to mankind to overcome evil with good in order to triumph over Satan's temptations to lure us to the wrong path.

Part of this test is to understand the nature of our existence. Energy is but one of the wonders of Creation, and we often taken it for granted. It is from this vantage point that I pursued an unending search for the many facets of energy and its impact on life. To understand how energy plays a vital role in sustaining life and connecting our spiritual entity to the Creator. As we undertake the test that God has given us, it makes sense to learn to understand how we can control and benefit from the energy that sustains us. How we utilize this flow of energy can provide us with the tools to improve our way of life in the direction of the straight path.

My parents have nurtured me with the tools of energy to better prepare myself for that test. By writing this book, I have become more aware of my own existence and purpose in life and the knowledge acquired to help make me a more unified Muslim. This book is dedicated to my parents, Haj Alie Turfe and Hajjah Hassaney Turfe, who were constant and steadfast in their faith and good deeds and an inspiration for me to pursue the study of Islam. This book is also dedicated to the Twelfth Imam, Imam Mohammad al-Mahdi, and may he pardon me for any errors I may have made.

1

ACKNOWLEDGMENTS

An American born, I had no formal training in Islamic studies. I self taught myself the Arabic alphabet at the age of twelve thereby enabling me to read the Qur'an in Arabic. The Qur'anic translations in English helped me to better understand the Arabic meaning. Each Sunday, for sixteen years, I taught the youth about the faith of Islam at the Islamic Center of America in Detroit, Michigan. This further strengthened my knowledge and understanding of Islam. I also gave lectures at the Islamic Center of America to adult groups, and I was often called upon to speak on Islam at churches and other institutions.

The growing Muslim community necessitated more Islamic centers, and I became more involved in studying, writing, and lecturing about Islamic topics. Religious scholars began to recognize my advanced level of Islamic knowledge, as they frequently called upon me to give presentations on Islam.

The eminent and renowned scholar, Sheikh Abdul Latif Berry, founder of the Islamic Institute of Knowledge in Dearborn, Michigan, mentored me to further enhance my knowledge and understanding of Islam and encouraged me to write books on Islam. This resulted in writing not only my books on *Patience in Islam: Sabr* and *Unity in Islam: Reflections and Insights* but also this book. I am very grateful to Sheikh Berry for opening my mind to the many facets of Islam as well as nurturing me to explore the depths of the philosophy in Islam. Sheikh Berry always encouraged me to utilize my knowledge, talents, and skills to undertake the study of contemporary facets of Islam for the purpose of enlightening the educated American Muslims. My book, *Patience in Islam: Sabr,* was selected by the highly acclaimed and world-renowned Islamic Jurisprudence Encyclopedia Institute for its library in Iran.

ABOUT THE AUTHOR

Haj Tallal Turfe was born in Detroit, Michigan on April 19, 1940. He is the son of Haj Alie Turfe and Hajjah Hassaney Turfe. He has four brothers, Bennett, Haj Fouad, Feisal, and Atallah, and one sister, Hajjah Wanda Fayz. His wife is Hajjah Neemat Turfe, and they have four sons, Alie, Haj Norman, Robert, and Haj Hassan, and one daughter, Summer Charara. Two of his sons graduated from the United States Military Academy at West Point. This achievement is a first for a Muslim to have entered and graduated from that Academy. That institution has produced the greatest American generals, and it also was the school from which some of America's presidents graduated.

Tallal is President and Chief Executive Officer of Premier Health Group LLC, an international firm providing short-range and long-range strategic solutions for healthcare clients in the Middle East and Africa. Some of the projects are the complete implementation of hospitals that include architectural/design, construction, equipment planning, and management. In addition, the company is engaged in implementing a complete diabetes medical center in the Middle East as well as providing diabetic medical supplies, orthotics/prosthetics for disabled people, and pharmaceuticals, medical equipment and supplies, and insurance/reinsurance healthcare plans.

Previously, Tallal was a Client Relationship Executive for 10 years with Diamond Management and Technology Consultants, a leading global management consultant firm. His focus was on strategic use of technology to gain new market opportunities, competitive advantages, cost reduction, and operational efficiencies for Fortune 500 companies.

Earlier, Tallal spent over 40 years in the automotive industry (Ford Motor Company and General Motors Corporation). During that period, he held various positions in industrial relations, purchasing, production control, export-import, marketing, trade relations, business planning, product planning and development, competitive intelligence, decision-making and risk analysis, geo-demographic information systems, and corporate strategy. Tallal has interacted with heads of states in the Middle East and Africa while employed with General Motors Corporation, and played a strategic role in the assembly operations in Egypt and Tunisia. He also generated hard currency for General Motors Corporation by countertrading products and services for third-world developing countries. He interacted with General Motors automotive dealers throughout the Middle East and provided strategic initiatives for moving product in the region. In 1978, Tallal authored a strategic white paper on the practical aspects of marketing automotive vehicles in Saudi Arabia.

5

Additionally, he is a professor at several universities such as the University of Michigan, Wayne State University, Eastern Michigan University, Central Michigan University, and the University of Windsor (Canada). On a part-time basis since 1969, he taught graduate and undergraduate courses in the field of business administration with concentration primarily in the disciplines of marketing, management, and business policy. A prolific writer, he has published several marketing and finance articles in leading business journals as well as two books, one entitled *Patience in Islam: Sabr*, written in Arabic, English, French, and Indonesian, and another entitled *Unity in Islam: Reflections and Insights*, written in English. Both of these books are on the "best seller" list, and have received high acclaim in the global arena.

Tallal is a board member of the American Task Force for Lebanon, a Washington, D.C.-based group engaged in facilitating the peace process and reconstruction in Lebanon. He has served on the board of directors of the Citizens Council for Michigan Public Universities, the Oakwood Healthcare System Foundation Strategic Board, the National Conference for Community and Justice (former chairman), and the American Red Cross. Currently, he serves on the board of directors of the Rehabilitation Institute of Michigan of the Detroit Medical Center, the Michigan Round Table for Diversity and Inclusion (former president), the Arab-American Chaldean Council (former chairman), the Henry Ford Community College Foundation, and the Advisory Council of Henry Ford Health System's Multicultural Dermatology. Tallal was also a member of former U.S. President Bill Clinton's *Call to Action: One America* race relations group. Dubai Television interviewed Tallal as one of the prominent and influential Arab Americans.

In August 2000, Tallal was one of 200 leaders of the world to be chosen by the United Nations to participate in the Millennium World Peace Summit. This Summit was held at the United Nations in New York, and it focused on four objectives: (a) conflict transformation; (b) forgiveness and reconciliation; (c) elimination of poverty; and (d) environmental preservation and restoration. Tallal was one of the signatories of the historical peace document.

In May 2003, Tallal was a keynote speaker at a global conference held at the United Nations headquarters in New York. The topic presented was *Islam's Perspective on Violence and Terrorism*. The purpose of the conference was to review and analyze the use of religion to incite for violence within the context of contemporary human rights and humanitarian laws. The conference took a major and essential step in filling the gap in international law and to restore peace, security, understanding and prosperity among the peoples of different faiths and cultures around the world.

Tallal has delivered three more presentations at the United Nations in New York: (1) *Education and Parenting for Peace and Global Ethics* (February 2004); (2) *Business Partners for Peace, Global Ethics and Public Diplomacy* (July 2004); and (3) *Protection of Religious Sites and Preventing the Use of Religion to Incite Terrorism/Violence* (December 2005).

Tallal is also a member of the Global Ethics Initiative, which is aligned with the United Nations. The Global Ethics Initiative advances and promotes the achievement of peace, the protection of children and the environment, and the promotion of ethics in all walks of life. Currently, the group is working on protecting the holy sites and historical sites as well as the tourists in the global arena.

For 50 years, Tallal has also been instrumental in securing gainful employment for thousands of people, mostly Middle Eastern but also Europeans, Asians, and South Americans as well as African-Americans from the Detroit Metropolitan Area – and this was done without a fee! For this achievement, his community gave a testimonial dinner in his honor in February of 1974. Another testimonial dinner was given in his honor in October of 1995, as he was the first Muslim to be presented with the *Knight of Charity Award* by the Vatican-based Pontifical Institute for Foreign Missions, an international community of Christian priests and lay missionaries who *maintain a preferential and evangelical option for the poor and marginalized of society*. Tallal was also inducted into the International Heritage Hall of Fame for his global humanitarian efforts, and his picture is permanently displayed on the wall of the Cobo Hall Center in Detroit, Michigan.

Tallal and his wife, Hajjah Neemat, have been instrumental in helping the youth in the Islamic community, particularly the Islamic Center of America and the Islamic Institute of Knowledge. They reinforce each other as examples of role models in volunteering their time to help those in need as well as to foster ethics and morals for the youth. Hajjah Neemat has done a great service to the community in also helping the elderly and medically impaired in the area of social services, for example, immigration, hospitals, and charitable endeavors. In addition, she also helps resolves family and personal problems among the youth and adults in the community.

ENERGY

by Tallal Alie Turfe

Life is but a force of energy,

That awakens our reality.

Energy the light for us to be,

As faithful Muslims in harmony.

Energy that soothes the conscious mind,

And dwells in the heart still to remind.

We answer the call to God's Decree,

With righteousness and serenity.

A test awakens our piety,

To answer His call for unity.

Holding steadfast to the strands that bind,

Strengthening the Rope to cleanse our mind.

It sparks the threads that lightens our soul,

As it paves the way to reach our goal.

Giving us strength and the will to see,

Our purpose in life through energy.

CONCEPTUAL FRAMEWORK

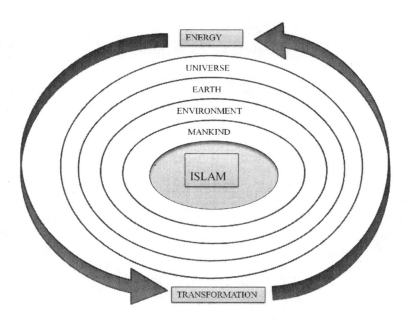

INTRODUCTION

When we gaze at the sky, we marvel at the myriad stars that light up the Heavens. Reflecting on this awesome display of creation, we cannot help but to appreciate not only the energy that drives this spectacle but, more importantly, the Creator who shaped it. Even to ponder on just one star, the sun, and how it provides sustenance to maintain the Earth's existence is amazing. As our knowledge increases about the nature and environment that nourish mankind, we discover that learning to overcome ignorance is a life-long endeavor.

The Universe is truly vast, and as we use our high-powered telescopes or spacecrafts to explore and navigate through it, we can further appreciate the Creator who put it all in place. However, there is no energy source capable to originate what we observe in the Universe. Only God has the power to create the Universe and all that is in it, for He is Omnipotent, Omniscient, and Omnipresent.

The study of energy has made significant inroads into the understanding of the Universe as well as of life itself. The study of energy has also shed light on how civilizations have advanced with their respective cultures, standards of living, and lifestyles. In addition, energy research has given us an innate appreciation for studying evolving environmental changes, as we trace the political, economic, social, and cultural conditions over the course of history. Energy has played a vital role in the transformation of societies and advancements in technology.

The purpose of this book is to capture just one aspect of God's creation – energy – and to examine its importance from an Islamic perspective. Toward this examination, we will discuss the concept of energy, as it applies to various facets of creation including mankind. Analogies will be drawn to show the similarities of energy forms and functions between mankind and the environment. We shall discuss how various forms of energy manifest themselves in Muslims performing their daily Islamic functions.

A thorough review will be made as to how energy in Islam interconnects with the philosophical criteria of consciousness and metaphysics. Additionally, a comprehensive examination and analysis will be made as to how energy transformed the Muslim community, with particular emphasis on the heroes of Islam who effectively used energy for the betterment of their communities and mankind.

While there have been a number of definitions of energy, the reality is that energy cannot be defined. However, there are characteristics of what energy is, for example, "the ability to do work," "the capacity for work or vigorous activity," and "usable heat or power." In short, there is no single definition that brings out all the characteristics of what energy is. Rather, energy

11

makes things happen and changes a condition. Energy is found in normal matter, such as atoms and molecules. Normal matter commonly exists in four states or phases: solid, liquid, gas, and plasma. The nature of energy is all around us. Energy flows through our senses. As the sun beams light, we can see energy. As the engine of a car is running, we can hear energy. As the wind touches our face, we can feel energy. As we eat food, we can taste energy. As we inhale the scent of a rose, we can smell energy. When we talk, we use energy. When we read a book, we use energy. When we swim, we use energy. Even when we sleep, we use energy.

Living organisms need energy for growth and movement. A lion needs energy to hunt. A plant needs energy to sprout. An eagle needs energy to soar. People use energy to work, while children use energy to play. Energy causes things to happen, whether the sun provides us light during the day or a street lamp lights our way at night. Energy heats our food, warms and cools our homes, powers our automobiles, airplanes, televisions, and computers. Even inanimate objects, such as stones, have energy. Rest assured, whatever we do is somehow connected to energy.

Whatever its shape and form, everything is energy. Each vibration is energy. Each atom or molecule is energy. The air we breathe and the water we drink are all energy. What we experience is impacted by energetic forces, for example, our thoughts and feelings as well as our emotions and physical well-being. Similarly, each word, thought, and action is energy.

This book will allow us to understand the importance of energy and how we can better use it to improve our health and lifestyle. Since the day we were born, we all have had practical experiences with energy. We often take life for granted not realizing that it is energy that is part and parcel of our lives. When asked as to what energy is, we have some understanding based on acquired knowledge and experience. Why are things the way they are? Why do we see the flash of lightning before we hear the sound of the thunder it makes? Why does water flow downhill but not uphill? How can a more thorough understanding of energy help us become better Muslims? It is my intent to shed light on these questions and the importance of energy as a life sustaining force.

ENERGY COMPOSITION OF THE UNIVERSE

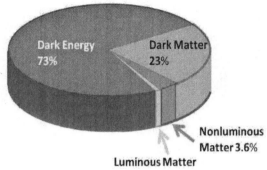

Dark Energy	Accelerates Rate of Expansion of Universe
Dark Matter	Slows Rate of Expansion of Universe
Luminous Matter & Nonluminous Matter	Consists of Protons, Neutrons & Electrons

Source: Wikipedia Encyclopedia

CHAPTER 1

CONCEPT OF ENERGY

The composition of the Universe consists of dark energy, dark matter, and normal matter (luminous matter and nonluminous matter).

Dark Energy

Dynamic and evolving in time, matter produces the Universe. About 96% of the matter in the Universe is dark and cannot be detected from the light it emits. A property of space, dark energy is an invisible energy that spreads through the entire Universe. It comprises about 73% of the energy composition of the Universe. Its negative gravity pushes galaxies apart.

This most abundant form of energy is also the most mysterious. No one knows what dark energy is or what causes it. As more space comes into existence, more dark energy would appear causing the Universe to expand faster. What this means is that objects that are expanding further away will be expanding even faster in the future; however, we don't know what causes this acceleration. Exploding stars indicate that the Universe was not just expanding but accelerating as well.[1] An example of dark energy is the supernova, which is a celestial spectacle involving the explosion of a star that is extremely bright releasing vast amounts of energy.

Dark Matter

Dark matter does not seem to emit detectable energy such as light. It is an invisible kind of matter that has a great deal of mass but appears not to radiate or reflect light of any kind. It cannot be detected directly, but we assume it exists because we see objects move, such as stars and galaxies. Therefore, while it is an undetected form of mass that emits little or no light, it is believed to exist because of its gravitational influence.[2]

It is believed that dark matter has positive gravity. Objects need additional gravity; otherwise, galaxies would fly apart. As it is not known from where this additional gravity comes from, scientists conclude that it is some invisible stuff, called dark matter. Its gravity governs the observed motions of stars and gas clouds. Dark matter comprises about 23% of the energy composition of the Universe.

An example of dark matter is a "black hole," which is a region of space in which the gravitational field is so powerful that nothing can escape its pull. Black holes are called black because we cannot see them, as no light emits from them. No light can reflect off of black holes, and they swallow all matter and all light that approaches them. Most black holes are believed to come about from the death of massive stars.

Normal Matter

Normal matter is also referred to as ordinary matter and consists of luminous matter and nonluminous matter. Although normal matter comprises only about 4% of the energy composition of the Universe, it consists of atoms that make up stars, planets, and every other visible object in the Universe. Normal matter is what atoms and molecules are made of. Atoms are the smallest units of normal matter, such as carbon, hydrogen, oxygen, and nitrogen. Molecules are made up of atoms.

Normal matter is everything we see and interact with, as atoms are made up of protons, neutrons, and electrons. Protons and neutrons are formed in a core nucleus, with electrons circulating outside. Normal matter is anything that has both mass and volume and occupies space. For example, an automobile would be said to be made of normal matter, as it occupies space and has mass. Normal matter commonly exists in four states or phases: solid, liquid, gas, and plasma.

Solid Phase

Solids have a definite shape, definite volume, high density, and very slight contraction and expansion, as atoms or molecules are held close together and tightly in place with little movement between them. Examples of solids are books, erasers, knives, ice (solid water), and floors.[3]

Liquid Phase

Liquids have an indefinite shape, definite volume, high density, and slight expansion and contraction, as atoms or molecules have more space between them, remain together, and move relatively freely than a solid does, but less than a gas, i.e., it is more fluid. Examples of liquids are water, blood, oil, milk, and coffee.[4]

Gas Phase

Gases have an indefinite shape, indefinite volume, low density, and easy contraction and expansion, as atoms or molecules are moving essentially unconstrained in random patterns with varying amounts of distance been the particles. Examples of gases are air, oxygen, helium, and steam.[5]

Plasma Phase

Plasma lacks shape and cannot be classified as a solid, liquid, or gas. While plasma temperatures and densities range from relatively cool and tenuous to very hot and dense, ordinary solids, liquids, and gases are both electrically neutral and too cool or dense to be in a plasma state. Atoms or molecules become increasingly ionized. Plasma is often referred to as an ionized gas, which is similar to a normal gas, except that electrons have been stripped from their respective nucleons and float freely within the plasma. As such, free electrons move among positively charged ions.

Plasma is by far the most common form of visible matter in the Universe, both by mass and volume. All the stars are made of plasma. Examples of plasma are the sun, lightning, comet tails, welding arcs, solar winds, fluorescent lights, neon signs, and the empty vastness of space. Products manufactured using plasmas impact our daily lives, such as computer chips, electronics, automobile parts, machine tools, and safe drinking water.[6]

Matter and Energy

In the Universe, everything is made up of matter and energy. Matter describes the physical things around us, such as the Earth, the air we breathe, or the automobiles we drive. Matter is everywhere. It is anything that has mass and takes up space. Everyone is made up of matter that is constantly experiencing both chemical and physical changes. Matter is made up of particles called atoms and molecules. Atoms are particles of elements – substances that cannot be broken down further. Atoms of elements can combine with one another to form compounds. Molecules are single units of compounds. For example, a glass of water contains many molecules of the compound water. Each molecule of water consists of two hydrogen atoms chemically combined with one oxygen atom.

As discussed earlier, there are four fundamental states of matter: solid, liquid, gas, and plasma. Matter is constantly changing, for example, if a snowman is put on the front lawn of a house with the outside temperature at 100 degrees Fahrenheit, then the snowman will melt because the outside temperature is higher than that of the snowman. Therefore, the ice that formed the snowman becomes liquid water. This is an example of a physical change, i.e., the solid water turned into liquid water.

Energy is the ability to cause change or do work. Any form of energy can be transformed into another form, but the total energy always remains the same. Some forms of energy include light, heat, electrical energy, and mechanical energy, such as movement. There are two states of energy: potential and kinetic. Potential energy is energy that is stored, while kinetic energy is energy in use. A detailed explanation of potential energy and kinetic energy will be discussed in the next chapter.

17

Energy and mater exist. Energy cannot be created or destroyed within our human power. Energy can turn into matter (particles) and then be destroyed back into energy. Scientists have proven that matter stores energy.[7] Different forms of energy, including heat, can change matter. Matter can change states through freezing, melting, evaporation, and condensation. Matter is all around us, in many different forms, and it can change. Matter is everywhere, such as in the air or in our hair. Even humans are matter, because they have volume and mass. Matter can be thought of as "stuff" and energy is "the stuff that moves stuff."[8] After the Big Bang, there was supposedly all energy, and that this energy became matter. In other words, energy was transformed into matter. Witness the transformation of energy into matter of a child in his mother's womb while she is pregnant.

Matter can be converted into energy, for example, nuclear fission. Matter is a form of energy. According to Einstein, energy can be converted into matter and vice versa, i.e., a great deal of energy is needed in the same place to make matter (E=MC2). Einstein's formula explains that matter and energy are interchangeable. E is energy that is equal to the mass of an object times the speed of light squared.[9]

Does energy derive from matter, or does matter derive from energy, or are both interchangeable? The discussion of matter and energy can become not only scientific and religious but philosophical as well. It is not my intent to resolve this age-old issue but merely to explain and illustrate the importance of energy in our lives.

Laws of Thermodynamics

First Law of Thermodynamics

The First Law of Thermodynamics (also known as the Law of Conservation of Energy) states that energy can neither be created nor destroyed; energy can only change forms; and in any process, total energy of the Universe remains the same.[10] Energy can be changed or transformed, for example, from chemical energy to heat energy. However, there is no observable change in the quantity of matter during a chemical reaction or a physical change. For example, a nuclear reactor changes energy from fuel into heat, which is then converted into mechanical energy that can be used to do work; however, the total amount of energy and matter remains constant. Likewise, the total amount of energy and matter also remains constant in the Universe.

Nasir al-Din al-Tusi (1201 AD – 1274 AD), a Muslim scientist, stated an early version of the law of conservation of mass. He wrote that a body of matter is able to change, but is not able to disappear. He said, "A body of matter cannot disappear completely. It only changes its form, condition, composition, color, and other properties, and turns into a different complex or elementary matter."[11]

18

The First Law of Thermodynamics does not contradict the Qur'an concerning the creation of the Heavens and Earth:

"We created the Heavens and the Earth and all between them in six periods...." (Qur'an 50:38)

"And the Heaven, We did raise it up with our might, and verily We are the expanders of expanse; and the Earth, We did spread it out like a carpet, how excellent are We the spreaders thereof." (Qur'an 51:47-48)

This verse makes it very clear that the "expanse" is the Universe, and that the Universe is becoming wider and more spacious. The size of the Universe is expanding and extending further and further. In this expansion, galaxies are constantly moving not only away from us but also from each other. Science and religion (Islam, Judaism, Christianity, Hinduism, and Buddhism) agree on the expansion of the Universe. Additionally, scientists have confirmed the existence of Dark Energy, which states that the Universe is expanding at an increasing rate.

The Big Bang Theory is substantiated by the Qur'an:

"Do not the unbelievers see that the Heavens and the Earth were joined together (as one unit of creation), before we clove them asunder? We made from water every living thing. Will they not then believe?" (Qur'an 21:30)

Here we note that the Universe was a single entity, and then it was separated by a powerful force, a powerful bang or explosion. As such, matter and space were once joined together as one and then separated by the explosion. The Big Bang Theory only substantiates what was already known in the Qur'an fourteen centuries earlier.

Second Law of Thermodynamics

The Second Law of Thermodynamics states that energy systems have a tendency to increase their entropy (disorder) rather than decrease it, and that heat can flow from a higher-temperature region to a lower-temperature region, but not the other way around.[12] In other words, the flow of heat will always be in one direction, i.e., from hot to cold. For example, the flow of heat of a metallic bar will always be in one direction, from warmer to colder, and will continue until the temperature of the entire bar becomes uniform. Another example is that an engine cannot transfer all of the heat energy from its fuel into mechanical energy; rather, it transfers some of the heat energy to colder objects.

There is no such thing as a perfectly efficient energy transformation. This means that energy transformations always tend to make systems less well ordered. Things left alone tend to drift into a lower energy state, i.e., a more disorganized form. A system reaches maximum entropy (disorder) when all order and energy are lost, for example, non-useful heat that is inoperative.

The Second Law supports the creation of the Universe and eventual termination of the Universe. The Qur'an states that the Universe had a beginning and it will have an end:

"...There is no God but He: all things are perishable but He...." (Qur'an 28:88)

According to Islam, the Universe was created by God. It is God who both expands and terminates the Universe. All will perish but God, for He is Everlasting, Permanent, and Self-Existent. The Universe is an irreversible path of entropy (disorder) leading to its ultimate elimination. Therefore, the Universe will ultimately expire, which means all objects in the Universe will exhaust their fuel and become dark and cold.

The Second Law of Thermodynamics states that all energy is proceeding towards uniformity and neutrality. The Universe has a beginning and will not exist forever. Even with the notion of the Big Bang Theory, there had to be a force to cause that explosion. That force is God. And it is God who will bring the Universe to its termination. According to the Laws of Thermodynamics, as everything will be at the same extremely low temperature, the Universe will continue to weaken until such time that energy will no longer be available and life would cease to exist.

Big Bang Theory – Islam and Science

Among the great religions of the world, the only Divine scripture that mentions and accepts the concept of the Big Bang Theory is the Qur'an:

Acceptance or Rejection of the Big Bang Theory

(Divine Scripture and Theologians)

Religion	Divine Scripture	Theologians (Pre 20th Century)	Theologians (Post 20th Century)
Islam	Yes	Yes	Yes
Christianity	No	No	Divided
Judaism	No	No	Divided
Hinduism	No	No	Divided
Buddhism	No	No	Divided

Source: Data derived from bibles and literature.

Islam has always accepted the concept of the Big Bang Theory, and it is so described in the Qur'an, which preceded scientific discoveries of the Big Bang Theory by over fourteen centuries. However, theologians of each of the Christian, Jewish, Hindu and Buddhist religions are divided, as some accept while others reject the Big Bang Theory. It is interesting to note that theologians, other than Muslims, did not accept the Big Bang Theory prior to the 20th Century; many have since come to accept it due to scientific discoveries.

The Big Bang Theory states that the Universe began as a single cosmic explosion about 15 billion years ago. The energy left over from the Big Bang is evenly spread out throughout the Universe. There has been mixed viewpoints as to the origin of the Universe. The issue of the creation of the Universe has always been associated with the concept of God. Some scientists believe the Universe was created out of the Big Bang Theory, while other scientists do not share this view. The theists took the Big Bang Theory as clear evidence for the creation of the Universe by God.

However, according to Eric Lerner and Michael Ibison and dozens of other scientists around the world, they refute that the Big Bang Theory relies on a growing number of hypothetical entities, things that we have never observed – inflation, dark matter, and dark energy are the most prominent examples – and without them there would be a fatal contradiction between the observations made by astronomers and the predictions of the Big Bang Theory.

These dissidents state that the Big Bang Theory can boast of no quantitative predictions that have subsequently been validated by observation.[13]

In response to these dissidents of the Big Bang Theory, Dr. George Smoot and Dr. John Mather proved that the Big Bang Theory did happen. They were awarded the 2006 Nobel Prize in physics for their research that verified the Big Bang Theory. They led a large team of scientists that demonstrated via the Cosmic Background Explorer (COBE) satellite that the radiation is precisely of the form that would be expected as a result of a Big Bang creation of the Universe. Dr. Mather was the driving force behind the COBE project, while Dr. Smoot was responsible for measuring small variations in temperature of the radiation. Dr. Smoot's findings essentially silenced the scientific critics of the Big Bang Theory and helped change the course of future investigations into the origin and evolution of the Universe.

Dr. Smoot and his research team produced maps of the entire sky that showed hot and cold regions with temperature differences of a hundred-thousandth of a degree. These temperature fluctuations, produced when the Universe was smaller than a single proton, were consistent with Big Bang predictions and are believed to be the primordial seeds from which grew our present Universe. Measurements made using Differential Microwave Radiometers (DMR), that Dr. Smoot and his team designed and built, provided the strongest scientific evidence yet that the Big Bang Theory is correct. "The tiny temperature variations discovered are the imprints of tiny ripples in the fabric of space-time put there by the primeval explosion process. Over billions of years, the smaller of these ripples have grown into galaxies, cluster of galaxies, and the great voids in space."[14]

In his article, *The Qur'an on the Expanding Universe and the Big Bang Theory,* Sherif Alkassimi provides an historical analysis in support of the Big Bang Theory. In 1916, Albert Einstein formulated his General Theory of Relativity that indicated that the Universe must be either expanding or contracting. Confirmation of the expanding-Universe theory finally came in 1929 in the hands of the well-known American astronomer Edwin Hubble. By observing red shifts in the light wavelengths emitted by galaxies, Hubble found that galaxies were not fixed in their position; instead, they were actually moving away from us with speeds proportional to their distance from Earth (Hubble's Law). The only explanation for this observation was that the Universe had to be expanding.

Soon after Hubble published his theory, he went on to discover that not only were galaxies moving away from the Earth, but were also moving away from one another. This meant that the Universe happened to be expanding in every direction, in the same way a balloon expands when filled with air. Hubble's new findings placed the foundations for the Big Bang Theory. The Big Bang Theory states that around 12 to 15 billion years ago the Universe came into existence from one single extremely hot and dense point, and that something triggered the explosion of this point that brought about the beginning of the Universe. The Universe, since then, has been expanding from this single point.

Later, in 1965, radio astronomers Arno Penzias and Robert Wilson made a Noble Prize winning discovery that confirmed the Big Bang Theory. Prior to their discovery, the theory implied that if the single point from which the Universe came into existence was initially extremely hot, then remnants of this heat should be found. This remnant heat is exactly what Penzias and Wilson found. In 1965, Penzias and Wilson discovered a 2.725 degree Kelvin Cosmic Microwave Background Radiation (CMB) that spreads through the Universe. Thus, it was understood that the radiation found was a remnant of the initial stages of the Big Bang. Presently, the Big Bang Theory is accepted by the vast majority of scientists and astronomers.[15]

Muslims share many common themes and beliefs with Christians, for example, the belief of an Omniscient, Omnipotent, and Omnipresent God. Unlike Christianity, science is compatible with Islam. Traditionally, religion and science are thought to be incompatible, because religion deals with faith and fundamental truths, whereas science deals with experimentation and hypotheses. However, Islam encourages the quest for knowledge that includes science. Over the centuries, Muslim scientists have done much to transform our knowledge of physics, medicine, mathematics, and philosophy.

While there are a number of Islamic institutions that promote the scholarly approach to understanding Islam and science, one such group has made significant inroads towards this understanding. The Hazara Society for Science Religion Dialogue in Pakistan is a non-profit society established with the efforts of learned and energetic teachers of colleges and universities of Hazara Division who are well-versed both in natural sciences and religion. Its main objective is to engage scholars from diverse disciplines for constructive, meaningful and purpose-oriented dialogue between religion and science. It has provided a forum where both traditionalists and modernists are invited, diverse viewpoints are presented and accommodated, and where tolerance is nurtured in its true spirit in religious scholars and scientists. One such scholar, Professor Faheem Ashraf, addressed the forum on the topic of "Islamic Concept of Creation of Universe, Big Bang and Science-Religion Interaction."

Professor Ashraf gives us a chronological insight into the Big Bang Theory, and he provides a detailed discussion and supporting verses from the Qur'an as to how the Big Bang came into existence. While scientific discoveries have always challenged the beliefs of all religions, Professor Ashraf engages in a discourse on Islam's view regarding the creation of the Universe, and how Muslim scholars have responded to the challenges and implications that have been posed by the Big Bang Theory and modern science.

According to the Qur'an, the Universe is solely created by God:

"...God is the Creator of all things: He is the One, the Supreme and Irresistible." (13:16)

23

"We created not the Heavens and the Earth and all between them but for just ends, and for a term appointed: but those who reject faith turn away from that whereof they are warned." (46:3)

This verse clearly rejects any notion of an eternal Universe that other theories, like the Steady State Theory, holds. Following are additional verses from the Qur'an that substantiate the creation:

"He said: 'So (it will be): thy Lord said, 'That is easy for Me: I did indeed create thee before, when thou had been nothing!'" (19:9)

"Do not the unbelievers see that the Heavens and the Earth were joined together (as one unit of creation), before We clove them asunder? We made from water every living thing. Will they not then believe?" (21:30)

"Moreover He comprehended in His Design the sky, and it had been (as) smoke: He said to it and to the Earth: 'Come ye together, willingly or unwillingly.' They said: 'We do come (together), in willing obedience.' So He completed them as seven firmaments in two periods, and He assigned to each Heaven its duty and command. And We adorned the lower Heaven with lights, and (provided it) with guard. Such is the Decree of (Him) the Exalted in Might, full of knowledge." (41:11-12)

There are some features of the Big Bang Theory that are closely similar to the Islamic concept of the creation of the Universe, for example, creation out of nothingness, initial singularity, concept of formation of galaxies from primordial gases, and uniformity of the Universe on a large scale. We have seen that the Islamic concept of the creation of the Universe is not contrary to some of the present scientific theories; in fact, these theories have enhanced our understanding of the Universe. This enhanced knowledge of the Universe has also improved our understanding of the Qur'an and Hadith (Traditions).[16]

The preceding explanation of the Universe and the Big Bang Theory is comprehensively demonstrated in the following sermon given by Imam Ali Ibn Abi Talib over fourteen centuries ago:

"God initiated all creation from void; originated it from non-existence. Neither did He need a power of intellect nor previous experience, neither movement nor thinking. To everything He assigned a term of life; He harmonized its particles, gave it its properties and its form. He knew each and every creation before its very existence. He knew its limitation, its end, its shape and form. He created the spheres, the distances, the celestial systems and the winds. He created water with turbulent currents, mounting waves, and passed over it stormy winds and mighty hurricanes. He ordered the wind to shed back the water, so the air gave way to the rain which fell in torrents. He also created sterile wind which He unleashed continuously and vigorously

and spread far and wide. He ordered the wind to intensify its motion and to stir the waters and waves in the oceans. It churned them like curd, and mixed them violently and continuously. So that the foam was carried by the wind, high up into the sphere. God created the seven skies, the lowest of which He made in the shape of stationary waves, the highest as a heavenly dome and a protective cover, without support or joints. He ornamented the skies with stars and planets. Among our constellations which He put into motion, He made the sun as a source of light and the moon to illuminate at night. "[17]

Kalam Cosmological Argument

As the Big Bang had to have an initial cause, Muslim philosophers addressed this issue. Al-Kindi (801 AD – 873 AD) is the first Muslim philosopher who advanced and used the Kalam Cosmological Argument for the existence of God. In his book, *On First Philosophy (Fi al-Falsafah al-Ula)*, he states that the Kalam Cosmological Argument rests on the premise that the Universe is not infinite in the past, but had a finite beginning that necessitates a cause for its existence. In other words, everything has a cause, that there must have been a first cause, and that this first cause was uncaused. Al-Kindi argues that "the noblest part of philosophy" is "the First Philosophy," and that is the "knowledge of the First Truth Who is the cause of all truth." He concludes that, "The True One is, therefore, the First, the Creator Who holds everything He has created, and whatever is freed from His hold and power reverts and perishes."[18] In summary, his proof is as follows:

1. The Universe has a beginning in time.

2. The Universe could not cause itself to come into existence.

3. Multiplicity in the Universe must be caused.

4. The cause of multiplicity in the Universe is the cause of the Universe itself, and it is the True One.[19]

Since everything that begins to exist has a cause of its existence, and since the Universe began to exist, therefore, the Universe has a cause of its existence. This cause is something beyond it and greater than it. The argument that everything that exists or occurs must have had a cause was earlier set forth by Plato and Aristotle in the 4th and 3rd Centuries BC. The Kalam Cosmological Argument was developed by Muslim philosophers in the Middle Ages, and has received great support from philosophers over the centuries. The word "Kalam" literally means "speaking," but can also mean "theological philosophy."[20]

During the last century, the Kalam Cosmological Argument has received great attention and support from Christian philosophers. Among the proponents of the Kalam Cosmological

Argument are Dr. Stuart C. Hackett, Dr. William Lane Craig, and Dr. Mark R. Nowacki. Dr. Stuart C. Hackett is a former Professor of Philosophy at Wheaton College and now Professor of Philosophy of Religion at Trinity Evangelical Divinity School. The Kalam Cosmological Argument was addressed in Dr. Hackett's book, *The Resurrection of Theism: Prolegomena to Christian Apology*, published in 1957.[21]

However, the defense of the Kalam Cosmological Argument came from one of Dr. Hackett's students, William Lane Craig, who first published *The Kalam Cosmological Argument* in 1979 and a subsequent edition in 2000. Dr. Craig is a Christian philosopher, both from scientific and philosophical perspectives. He is a research professor of philosophy at Talbot School of Theology at Biola University, a nationally ranked private Evangelical Christian university located in California. Dr. Craig has authored or edited over thirty books. He is an international speaker at numerous universities, including Harvard, Princeton, Yale, Stanford, Oxford, Cambridge, Moscow, and Peking. He supports the Kalam Cosmological Argument, which leads to a personal Creator of the Universe. He is credited with reviving the Kalam Cosmological Argument, which argues for a first cause from the finitude of past events and the origin of the cosmos.

Dr. Craig holds the position that since the Universe began to exist, the efficient cause of the Universe's existence must have been God. His modern version of the Kalam Cosmological Argument, first formulated by the Mutakallimeen, the Muslim scholastics of the Ninth Century, rests on empirical arguments as well as a priori considerations that an actual infinite is impossible. Since an actual infinite is impossible, Dr. Craig argues, the Universe must, therefore, be finite in time. In other words, the Universe must have begun to exist. In reaching the conclusion to God as the Universe's cause, Dr. Craig relies upon the Muslim "principle of determination," first argued by al-Juwayni (1028 AD – 1085 AD) and later by al-Ghazali (1058 AD – 1111 AD) and Averroes (Ibn Rushd) (1126 AD – 1198 AD). The "principle of determination" states that any being or effect requires a "particularizer," a being who decides the course of an action between two likely choices.[22] What distinguishes the Kalam Cosmological Argument from other forms of cosmological arguments is that it rests on the idea that the Universe has a beginning in time.

Dr. Mark R. Nowacki is a former Professor of Philosophy at George Washington University and Howard University and now Professor of Philosophy at Singapore Management University. A book entitled, *The Kalam Cosmological Argument for God*, was authored by Dr. Nowacki and published in 2007.[23] This book supports and validates the findings of Dr. Craig as well as that of the Muslim philosophers of ancient times.

Commentary

In their book, *Philosophy of Islam*, Dr. M. Husayni Behishti and Dr. M. Jawad Bahonar give the following account of the creation:

"*Through observation, experiment, and calculation, man has found that the world is well-organized. There exist definite relations between its elements and its phenomena, and it is governed by firm laws...existence of this systematic organization is so definite that no natural event is considered to be haphazard and having no relation with other phenomena...the world with all its dimensions has systematic interrelations at all levels, which are so precise and complex that they are evidently well-calculated.*"

"*The harmony and methodical composition found in millions of natural phenomena require a suitable factor. For its growth, a plant requires the necessary quantity of the mixture of soil, rain water, solar energy, and air components, so that it may bloom and blossom. Which is the power that arranges this working together, mutual attraction, and mutual influencing? Why do various elements, in a precise quantity and under specific conditions, come together to produce the required affect?*"

"*Science has rendered a great service by discovering that there is nothing accidental and haphazard...no simple or compound matter and no closed system can ever make itself without outside help. Similarly, no collection of various kinds of matter and no group of systems has the power of creating and managing any orderly, well-arranged motile and evolutionary arrangement or system. For this purpose, every kind of matter individually and even collectively requires some outside contact and help. As it is now evident that such an arrangement cannot emerge automatically from within matter, we must look for outside factor to explain its existence, and as we know that the existing arrangement is well-calculated and orderly, that factor must have consciousness and will to create it.*"

"*Our world is that of union, where things come together either to combine or to dissolve...discovery of natural laws does not mean that we no longer need a law-giver and designer of nature. The force which, through the power of contradiction, has produced billions of galaxies and other marvelous natural phenomena from matter is in itself a sign that there exists a cognizant guidance and wise consciousness, which has put in matter the power of creating such an orderly arrangement and has brought about such a well-calculated world.*"

"*Islam regards this world with all its greatness, vastness, and marvels and all the interconnections between its various phenomena as a homogenous reality dependent upon another Reality which is Independent, Sovereign, and Supreme. We call this Independent Reality God. Like all other imperceptible realities, He is recognized by His perceptible Signs. It is through these Signs that we obtain valuable and fruitful knowledge of Him.*"[24]

27

Energy and the Earth

By the Grace of God, the Earth provides the sustenance necessary for mankind's survival. In addition to the many elements needed for survival, God also provided mankind with water, plants, animals, and inanimate beings. Without air, we would not survive. Without water, we would not survive. Without the sun, there would be no light. Without plants and animals, there would be no nourishment for our bodies. Everything that was bestowed upon us by God was done in proportion to our needs.

The main challenge for mankind is to preserve all that God has provided. Not only did God provide us with the Earth but the Universe as well, in order to benefit from and make use of it. As God has provided us with the balance in nature, it is our responsibility and accountability to maintain and preserve that balance. As man evolved over the centuries, he introduced technology that made it easier and more practical to reap their needs and wants from the natural environment. For example, the use of materials to provide clothing and shelter enabled man to increase his standard of living.

The Earth is abundant in energy resources, and man has used these sources of energy to fuel their homes, facilitate the modes of transportation, construct dams, improve living conditions for animals, find alternative uses for plants such as medicine, and the myriad of other uses that derive from the natural environment. As such, mankind strives to be in perfect harmony with the purpose of their existence.

According to the Qur'an, the balance of the environment is revealed in the atmosphere that surrounds it:

"And the Firmament has He raised high, and He has set up the balance (of justice), in order that you may not transgress (due) balance. So establish weight and justice and fall not short in the balance." (Qur'an 55:7-9)

Balance must be maintained, for example, relative to the abundance of gases in the atmosphere. The percentage volume of these gases in the atmosphere are nitrogen (78.03%), oxygen (20.99%), carbon dioxide (0.03%), and argon, helium, neon, etc. (0.95%). All these gases are necessary for mankind to survive, and survival depends on maintaining the balance of these ratios. The air is mostly made up of nitrogen and oxygen (99.02%). The ratio of nitrogen must be sustained in order to balance the harmful and burning effects of oxygen. Oxygen is required for all animal life on Earth from humans to bacteria for respiration (breathing). Oxygen helps burn up food and converts it into energy in our bodies. Carbon is in the air in the form of carbon dioxide. Carbon dioxide is required by plant life for photosynthesis, the process of using sunlight to create simple sugars (energy) the plants need to grow and live. This process of

28

photosynthesis by plants also releases oxygen that animal life needs. One important property of carbon dioxide is its ability to absorb infrared radiation (heat) and reradiate it. This is the carbon problem also known as Global Warming. Carbon in the air as carbon dioxide comes from a variety of sources, for example, volcanoes and the burning of carbon based materials for energy such as coal, oil, and wood.[25]

ENERGY USES
(SELECTED EXAMPLES)

Radiant

Electrical

Chemical

Sound

Thermal

Nuclear

Mechanical

Magnetic

CHAPTER 2

FORMS OF ENERGY

Energy Defined

Although the popular definition of energy is "the ability to do work," it does not really fit in with what we know about thermodynamics. Perhaps, there is not a single definition that brings out all the characteristics of what energy is. While "the ability to do work" is characteristic of energy, it is only one of a number of characteristics of energy.

Various dictionary sources have defined energy as "the ability to do work" but also as "the capacity for work or vigorous activity" as well as "usable heat or power." Work is the transfer of energy through motion. The amount of work done depends on the amount of force exerted and the distance over which the force is applied. Work can be calculated by using the following formula: work equals force times distance.

While these definitions of energy have been used by scholars, scientists, and students, they really do not define energy. In reality, no one knows what energy is. For example, "the ability to do work" is more of a characteristic of energy than a definition. Perhaps, a better explanation of energy is that which makes things happen.

Energy is a characteristic of matter that makes things happen. When things happen, there is a changed condition, for example, volume, temperature, and pressure. If solid changes into liquid or liquid changes into vapor, something happened, i.e., there is a change in condition. If there is no energy, then nothing would ever change or happen. Therefore, energy changes whenever anything happens. For example, if a tea kettle is placed on a heated stove, the water would begin to boil making the water turn into steam. There is a change in condition, as energy is transferred through the flow of heat. Energy also flows when the cup of tea cools down resulting in a changed condition.

Kinetic Energy and Potential Energy

Thermodynamics tells us that energy cannot be created, destroyed, or recycled. Energy entering or leaving the atmosphere determines the Earth's climate. Energy from the sun creates conditions necessary for life. Energy is harnessed to support and improve life. Energy is the driver of environmental change and human health. Energy balance enhances Islamic well-being,

31

while energy imbalance diminishes Islamic well-being. The two states of energy are kinetic energy and potential energy.

Kinetic energy is the energy of motion or energy possessed by a moving object. An object that has motion, whether it is vertical motion or horizontal motion, has kinetic energy. It is motion of waves, electrons, atoms, molecules, substances, and objects.

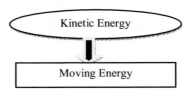

- Eating & Walking
- Talking & Swimming

Examples of kinetic energy would be a speeding automobile, thrown baseball, or downpour of a waterfall. Electrical energy is the movement of electrical charges. Radiant energy is electromagnetic energy that travels in transverse waves. Thermal energy, or heat, is the internal energy in substances and the vibration and movement of the atoms and molecules within substances. Motion energy is the movement of objects and substances from one place to another.[26]

Potential energy is energy stored in matter. Potential energy exists whenever an object that has mass has a position within a force field, for example, the position of objects in the Earth's gravitational field.

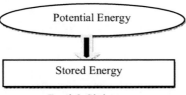

- Food & Sitting
- Gasoline & Idling

An example of potential energy is chemical energy, which is stored in the bonds of atoms and molecules; it is the energy that holds these particles together. Another form of potential energy is mechanical energy, which is stored in objects by application of a force. Nuclear energy is another form of potential energy, as it is stored in the nucleus of an atom and holds the nucleus together.[27]

Let's see how both kinetic energy and potential energy can be applied to the same object, for example, a book. Pushing a book off a desk that falls to the floor results in motion, i.e., the moving book uses kinetic energy. By picking up the book and putting it back on the desk, one would use his own potential (stored) energy to lift the book and then to move (kinetic energy) the book. Moving the book higher than the floor adds energy to it. As the book is resting on the desk, means that the book has potential (stored) energy. Of course, if the book were placed on the shelf of a bookcase that is higher than the desk, then that means the book would have more potential energy. If the book should fall from the bookcase, which is higher than the desk, then that would mean that the book has more potential energy.

Stretching a rubber band necessitates potential energy. Once the rubber band is released, potential energy is changed to motion (kinetic energy). Any movement of the rubber band is kinetic energy. Another example of the interplay of potential energy and kinetic energy is the yo-yo. Holding the yo-yo toy stationary (motionless) in one's hands is potential energy, but as it starts to fall, the potential energy changes into kinetic energy. The yo-yo that is wound up has maximum potential (stored) energy, while the yo-yo that falls as far as it can has maximum kinetic (motion) energy. Yet another example is demonstrated by a frog. A frog sitting is an example of potential energy, while a frog leaping is an example of kinetic energy.

The two most common energy conversions are: potential energy changing into kinetic energy and kinetic energy changing into potential energy. Other energy conversions are: (a) chemical energy into heat energy; (b) heat energy into mechanical energy; (c) nuclear energy into heat energy; and (d) mechanical energy into electromagnetic energy.

Energy makes things happen. Heat energy drawn from the sun creates the conditions necessary for life. When we run, play, work, eat, or perform the myriad of other functions of the human body, we use energy. Relative to the Earth's climate, there is a balance of energy entering and leaving the atmosphere. Not only do plants and animals contain energy, they use energy as well. As such, energy can be found in a number of different forms: heat, chemical, nuclear, mechanical, and electromagnetic.

Avicenna (Ibn Sina) (980 AD – 1037 AD) is regarded as the father of early modern medicine. A Muslim, he was also a philosopher, mathematician, astronomer, chemist, physicist, theologian, statesman, and a poet. In his *Kitab al-Shifa (The Book of Healing)*, he wrote a composite work of philosophy and science. He synthesized Aristotelian and Neoplatonic thought with Islamic theology. His book also contains many original scientific ideas. He proposed a corpuscular theory of light, which implied a finite speed of light. He distinguished between different forms of heat and mechanical energy and contributed to the development of the concepts of force, infinity, and the vacuum. He also investigated the relationship between time and motion concluding that they must be interrelated, since time can have no meaning in a world devoid of motion. He introduced the notion that movement and motion within an object, such as the motion of atoms and molecules, is a form of thermal energy that produces heat. This concept has great relevance on the Laws of Thermodynamics, enthalpy, entropy, and chemical reactions.[28]

Heat Energy

The internal motion of the atoms is called heat energy, because moving particles produce heat. Heat energy can be produced by friction. Heat energy causes changes in temperature and phase of any form of matter. Heat is a form of energy that transfers among particles in a substance by means of kinetic energy of those particles. When heat is transferred by particles bouncing into each other, there is movement. That movement is kinetic energy. If two bodies at different temperatures are brought together, energy is transferred, i.e., heat flows from the hotter body to the colder body. The effects of this transfer of energy usually, but not always, is an increase in the temperature of the colder body and a decrease in the temperature of the hotter body.

Heat is given off when an object's thermal energy is transferred. Thermal energy can be transferred in three ways: by conduction, by convection, and by radiation. Conduction is the transfer of energy from one molecule to another. This transfer occurs when molecules hit against each other. Conduction takes place in solids, liquids, and gases. Convection is the movement of heat by a liquid such as water or a gas such as air. The liquid or gas moves from one location to another, carrying heat along with it. Heat travels from the sun by a process called radiation, which is the transfer of heat by electromagnetic waves. Examples of heat energy are gas stoves, water heaters, and gas heat.[29]

Chemical Energy

Chemical energy is possibly the easiest source of energy to obtain, and it is the most efficient form of energy to use and to store. It is also readily available, as we can find it in just about everything we use. Our food contains the chemical energy we need to live and grow.

Chemical energy is required to bond atoms together. When atoms are broken, energy is released. Fuel and food are forms of stored chemical energy. Chemical energy is the energy stored in the bonds of atoms and molecules. This is a form of potential energy until the bonds are broken. Fossil fuels and biomass store chemical energy. Products that contain chemical energy include: TNT, baking soda, body cells, batteries, and matches. Biomass, petroleum, natural gas, propane and coal are examples of stored chemical energy. In the example of a battery, energy is released because the chemicals inside are reacting to produce electrons needed to create electricity.[30]

Nuclear Energy

The nucleus of an atom is the source of nuclear energy. When the nucleus splits (fission), nuclear energy is released in the form of heat energy and light energy. Nuclear energy is also released when nuclei collide at high speeds and join (fuse). The sun's energy is produced from a nuclear fusion reaction in which hydrogen nuclei fuse to form helium nuclei. Nuclear energy is the most concentrated form of energy. Nuclear energy is the energy stored in the nucleus of an atom. Nuclear energy is unusual in that it can give off energy in the form of light or heat, but is the change in the atom's makeup that produces the energy. Submarines, power plants, atomic bomb, sun, stars, and smoke detectors all use nuclear energy. Nuclear power plants use uranium, a radioactive element, to create electricity.[31]

Mechanical Energy

When work is done to an object, it acquires energy. The energy is acquires is known as mechanical energy. When you kick a football, you give mechanical energy to the football to make it move. When you throw a bowling ball, you give it energy. When that bowling ball hits the pins, some of the energy is transferred to the pins (transfer of momentum). Mechanical energy is the movement of machine parts. Conversely, if the football, bowling ball, and machine parts are resting, then energy is being stored. That stored energy is potential energy. Mechanical energy is also the total amount of kinetic and potential energy in a system. Wind-up toys, grandfather clocks, cars, planes, wagons, and pogo sticks are examples of mechanical energy. Wind power uses mechanical energy to help create electricity. Potential energy plus kinetic energy equals mechanical energy.[32]

Electromagnetic Energy

Power lines carry electromagnetic energy into your home in the form of electricity. Light is a form of electromagnetic energy. Each color of light represents a different amount of electromagnetic energy. Electromagnetic energy is also carried by X-rays, radio waves, and laser light. Radiant energy is also called electromagnetic energy. Radiant energy is the movement of photons. All life on Earth is dependent on radiant energy from the sun. Examples of radiant energy include radio waves (AM, FM, TV), microwaves, X-rays, and plant growth. Active solar energy uses photovoltaic panels and light to turn radiant energy into chemical energy.[33]

Energy Needs and Uses

The body needs constant energy to do the work necessary to maintain life and health. The actions involved are both voluntary and involuntary. The energy needed requires fuel, provided in the form of nutrients, such as carbohydrates, fats, and proteins. Energy needs can be classified into low energy, medium energy, and high energy. Some examples of these energy needs are the following:

Low Energy	Medium Energy	High Energy
Reading	Walking	Running
Sitting	Golfing	Bicycling
Eating	Skating	Playing Soccer
Meditating	Bowling	Exercising

Low energy activities include at least an hour each day in one of the following: reading, sitting, eating, or meditating. Medium energy activities include at least an hour each day in one of the following: walking, golfing, skating, or bowling. High energy activities include at least an hour each day in one of the following: running, bicycling, playing soccer, or exercising. We need energy to do the things we do every day. When we eat food, our body can use the chemical energy in the food to make our muscles move so we can breathe, walk, run, and jump. The chemical energy in the food gets changed into the mechanical energy of moving muscles.

There have been numerous accomplishments in modern technology. In ancient times, humans could only harness the energy from their muscles and from fire. The agricultural revolution and industrial revolution were major forces in finding alternative ways to harness energy and make life more palatable for mankind. Just think, a century ago we didn't have central air conditioners to cool our homes, microwave ovens to heat our food, refrigerators to store our food, or televisions to entertain us. The use of lights has revolutionized the way we live, work, and play. Today, that technology is not only available but advancing to improve our living conditions.

While we are using energy at a staggering rate, we have to find ways to use less energy and to use it more wisely. Energy conservation and energy efficiency are the challenges we face. For example, recycling can save energy and natural resources through conservation. It takes less energy to make new cans from recycled scrap than it takes to make new cans from raw materials. Another example for conserving energy is to wash clothes by using less water and cooler water. Switching the temperature setting from hot to warm can cut a load's energy use in half. Energy efficiency allows us to use less energy to provide the same level of energy service, for example, by insulating a home to use less heating and cooling energy to achieve the same temperature.

How often do we hear someone say, "turn off the lights" or "conserve energy." The Law of Conservation of Energy states that the total amount of energy in a system remains constant, or conserved, although energy within the system can be changed from one form to another or transformed from one object to another.

We learn from the First Law of Thermodynamics that energy cannot be created or destroyed, but it can be transformed. This First Law of Thermodynamics is also known as the Law of Conservation of Energy, which means that when energy is being used, it is not being used up. Instead, it is being changed from one form to another. Stored energy uses can be thought of as potential energy, which can be converted into another state of energy, such as kinetic energy. The following illustrates how stored potential energy is used:

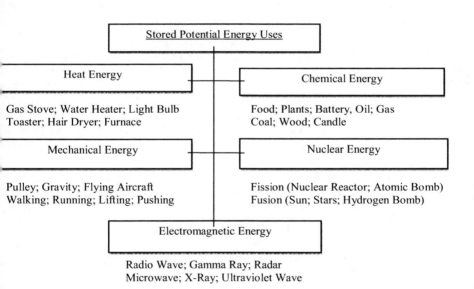

A battery contains chemical potential energy and when the energy is released, it can do work to power a flashlight. When you lift a bowling ball, you must do work against gravity. That work is transformed into gravitational potential energy that can be released as kinetic energy if you drop the ball. An automobile engine burns fuel, converting the fuel's chemical energy into mechanical energy to make the automobile move. The engine does not create the energy that powers an automobile. The engine is a machine that allows the stored chemical energy of gasoline to be transformed into mechanical energy that drives the wheels of the automobile. Windmills change the wind's energy into mechanical energy to turn turbines, which then produce electricity. Solar cells change sunlight, or radiant energy, into electrical energy.

When a candle is burning, chemical energy is converted to light energy (chemical to light), or chemical energy is converted to heat energy (chemical to heat). When the school bell is ringing, mechanical energy is converted to sound energy (mechanical to sound). Chemical energy is stored in foods and fuels, and can be released when these compounds undergo chemical reactions. Different types of stoves are used to transform the chemical energy of fuel (e.g., gas, coal, or wood) into heat energy. Hydroelectric plants transform the kinetic energy of falling water into electrical energy.

We note how energy is used in metabolism, which is the rate that the body turns food into energy. Metabolism is a set of chemical reactions that occur in living organisms in order to maintain life. Our bodies get the energy they need from food through metabolism, the chemical reactions in the body's cells that convert the fuel from food into the energy needed to do sustain our lives. In other words, food is chemical energy that can be captured through metabolic pathways and subsequently used to power the cellular functions in our bodies. People can have a slow or fast rate of metabolism. Metabolism is mandatory for all life forms, for example, plants and animals. In metabolism, biochemical reactions acquire and use energy. Organisms need and use energy in order to (a) combat entropy (disorder); (b) build new structures; (c) repair or break down old structures; and (d) reproduce. Consumers obtain energy and nutrients by eating other organisms.[34]

Other uses of energy are manifold. Energy from the sun gives us daylight. Energy lights our cities. Energy powers trains and airplanes. Energy powers vehicles through gasoline and diesel fuel. Energy warms our homes and heats our food. Energy powers machinery in factories. Energy provides heat, power, and light by way of electricity. Energy helps plants grow. Energy is used when we speak. Energy helps us prostrate in prayer.

The First Law of Thermodynamics states that energy can neither be created nor destroyed, but it can be changed into other forms of energy or matter. In other words, for every action there is an exchange of energy. When energy is used, it does not disappear. Energy is never consumed; it doesn't go away. It is conserved. It is constant. It only changes or moves. The total quantity of energy stays the same and must be accounted for. For example, for every 100 units of fuel energy that is burned in an engine, 100 units of converted energy have to go somewhere and do something. An object sitting upon the edge of a desk is potential energy. However, when the object falls, it will change form, i.e., kinetic energy. Then when the object is at rest, it will change back to potential energy. Another example is when a rubber band is stretched, potential energy is stored. However, when the rubber band is shot into the air, its kinetic energy is released. When finished, the energy returns to potential energy and is stored.

Measurement of Energy

There is no absolute measure of energy, because energy is characterized as the work that one system does (or can do) on another. Therefore, only of the transition of a system from one state into another can be defined and thus measured. However, David Watson provides an excellent understanding of energy. He cites the work of an English physicist, James Prescott Joule, who conducted experiments in the 1840's as to how energy behaves. Joule did a long series of experiments that showed that heat is a form of energy. Joule found the relationship between a unit of mechanical energy and a unit of heat. This helped Joule finalize what chemists and natural philosophers had come to believe – that the total energy in the Universe is constant, although energy is continuously changing forms:

"The knowledge that mechanical work could be converted to heat and that we could measure and predict how much heat would result from a given amount of work was a huge discovery. As a result, each unit of energy was named after Mr. Joule. It's called the Joule (J)."

"In the experiment, Joule simply attached a weight by pulley and string to some paddles in an insulated container of water. The weight turns the paddles as it falls. The turning paddles do work on the water (they push it all around, "churning it up") equal to the force of gravity on the weight times the distance (L) the weight is pulled down by the gravitational force. It's the formula for work – force time distance. By the time the weight stops, all of its potential energy at the start of the "fall" has been transferred by the work process into the water (minus a little friction in the pulley and ropes). What happened to the energy? If the First Law of Thermodynamics is true, it had to end up somewhere; it couldn't just disappear. Joule measured the water temperature and found the temperature had increased. The water was a little bit warmer because the mechanical work of the paddles had increased the energy level of the water molecules by pushing them around."

"Through experiments like this, Joule and others were able to determine the equivalent values of thermal energy and mechanical energy. This knowledge allows us to keep track of all the energy in complicated processes. For example, by knowing that a certain amount of work can be converted into a certain amount of heat, we are able to accurately account for all of the fuel's energy as it is converted in an engine. Measured carefully and accurately, all of the energy out does equal all of the energy in."[35]

The principle of energy conservation involved in Joule's work gave rise to the new scientific discipline known as thermodynamics. While Joule was not the first scientist to suggest the principle, he was the first to demonstrate its validity. Joule's principle of energy conservation formed the basis of the First Law of Thermodynamics, which states conclusively that the Universe did not create itself. The present structure of the Universe is one of conservation, not innovation as required by the theory of evolution.[36] While evolutionists cannot explain how this constant amount of energy/matter originated, the Qur'an does provide an explanation:

"...He created all things, and He hath full knowledge of all things." (Qur'an 6:101)

"He Who created the Heavens and the Earth and all that is between, in six periods...." (Qur'an 25:59)

ISLAMIC PRAYER & FASTING

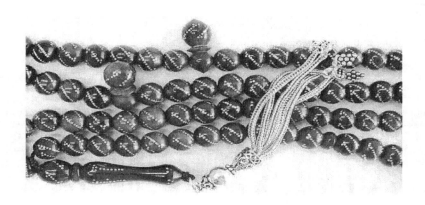

CHAPTER 3

APPLICATION OF
ENERGY FORMS IN ISLAM

Intention

"Verily it is We Who have revealed the Book to thee in truth; so serve God, offering Him sincere devotion. Is it not to God that sincere devotion is due?..." (Qur'an 39:2-3)

Is Islam, what is important is the purity of our intention (*niyyah*). The word *devotion* in this verse is tantamount to intention. What people think and feel underscore the essence of intention in Islam. Intention relative to our motives should always be in the direction of the satisfaction and approval of God. As a consequence, God evaluates our deeds according to the intentions behind them.

Before we begin our prayer, fast, devotion, action, or any Islamic obligation, we make our intention to do so. Intention requires energy to bring it into concentration. The energy is emotion. The intensity of emotional energy elevates our spirituality. The strength of our emotion brings about a strong intention. It is the extent or range of vibration rather than the frequency that determines the strength of intention. Increasing the emotion increases the extent of the vibration. Our thoughts and feelings are impacted by emotional energy. Our thought waves are like radio waves, in that the electromagnetic wave is the energy and the information transmitted is the content. Content is the data portion of a thought, and energy is the carrier that gives a thought the power to manifest. The more strongly we think and feel about something, the more energy we give to it.

Our intention sets the direction in which we are headed. An electric field cannot be transmitted through space by itself. In order to transmit an electric field, it must be integrated with a magnetic field, thus creating an electromagnetic field. The energy fields, or energy waves, which are transmitted through space from our television broadcasting station is electromagnetic in nature. Similarly, our electrical thought energy combines with our magnetic emotional energy to create an intention electromagnetic energy field that is constantly being radiated out in all directions from us, just like the energy from a television broadcasting antenna. Correspondingly, the heart is the electrical powerhouse of the human body. Each heartbeat begins with a pulse of electricity through the heart muscle. This electricity arises because a large number of charged particles flow across the muscle membranes to excite contraction. These charged ions are found throughout the body creating a whole circuitry system that joins to form an energy field that resonate our intention.

In making our intention to pray or fast, we must be absolute in stating our intention. It is not sufficient to simply make our intention and then forget about it. If one forgets to make his intention but is aware that the intention should have been made, then it is acceptable. Our intent energy field is an integrated energy field that includes both our thoughts and feelings. To express a thought in the form of a desire, without it being accompanied by deep and sincere

41

feelings, will not result in a clear intention. There also must be consistency between the desire we set in our intention energy field and the physical actions we take. Bringing discipline into our intention requires a shift in our awareness.[37] But intentions are only conscious mental states, if one is aware of having them. It is recommended to also make one's intention to include desirable and preferred acts of devotion in prayer and fast. For example, the call for prayers and fasting extra days are recommended and preferred (*mustahab*).

Each pulse of intention is an electrical spark, a powerful life current, an intention signal transmitted from us, outwardly, to seek the Blessing of God. Our Islamic faith is formed and shaped from a positive, powerful intention that is active. Rather than searching for our intention, we simply become that intention. Since the cells in our bodies march to the tune of consciousness, let intention be our life.

Prayer

"Only those believe in Our Signs, who, when they are recited to them, fall down in adoration, and celebrate the praises of their Lord, nor are they (ever) puffed up with pride." (Qur'an 32:15)

"Adoration" in this context means prostration, which is expressive of profound humility, faith, and gratitude to God. The benefits of prayer are many. In addition to the spiritual benefits of prayer, Muslims improve their digestive tract and metabolism, as well as increase their energy consumption. During prayer, kinetic energy (motion) helps increase the blood flow to the heart and strengthens the muscles in our body. Additional benefits in prayer are a decrease in fatigue, increased rate of breathing, uplift in emotional well-being, hygiene via ablution, and being more physically fit. Regular prayer also reduces cholesterol in the body. Prayer is an excellent form of exercise for the heart, as it supplies fresh blood to all body tissues. The importance of prayer also has many benefits to the cardiac, respiratory, skeletal, and muscular systems.

In addition to making one's intention to pray, ablution, recitation, and prostration (bowing and kneeling down) are mandatory requirements:

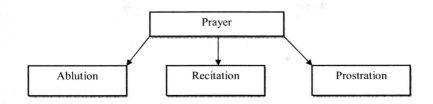

```
                    ┌──────────────────┐
                    │      Prayer      │
                    └──────────────────┘
          ┌──────────────┼──────────────┐
          ▼              ▼              ▼
  ┌────────────┐  ┌────────────┐  ┌──────────────┐
  │  Ablution  │  │ Recitation │  │ Prostration  │
  └────────────┘  └────────────┘  └──────────────┘
```

Ablution

"O you who believe! When you prepare for prayer, wash your faces, and your hands (and arms) to the elbows; rub your heads (with water); and (rub) your feet to the ankles...." (Qur'an 5:7)

Ablution is required before performing the prayer. Islam is based on cleanliness and, as such, ablution makes us clean and prepares us mentally for prayer. Ablution allows us to cool the nerves in our body in order to heighten our concentration as we humble ourselves before God. For example, when a person faints, water is sprinkled on his face and other parts of the body to awaken him. The same analogy can be made relative to ablution. Application of water to parts of our body awakens us, so our thoughts are in harmony with our consciousness of prayer.

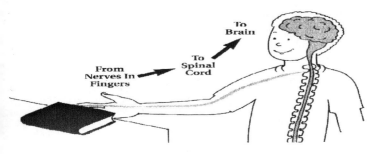

Source: © 1993 Children's Television Workshop

From touching the book in the picture above, we can note that electrical impulses generated in the fingers pass along the nervous system until picked up by the brain for processing. Impulses are also sent from the brain to other parts of the body. Every cell in the human body is electric, and electrical impulses control our muscles. Likewise, when we perform the ablution, the water we use to cleanse ourselves also generates electrical impulses throughout our body. These electrical impulses stimulate our brain to better prepare us to be more focused in prayer. Water is an excellent conductor of electrical energy. Water increases the efficiency of electrical and chemical actions between the brain and the nervous system.[38]

Ritual purity (*tahara*) is a requirement before proceeding to prayer. According to al-Ghazali (1058 AD – 1111 AD), an Islamic philosopher, Imam Ali Zein al-Abideen (Fourth Imam) used to turn pale when he made his ablution. When his family asked him what came over him during his ablution, he would say, "Do you realize before Whom I wish to stand in prayer?"[39]

The two types of ablution are *ghusl* (major ablution) and *wudhu* (minor ablution). *Ghusl* is a complete washing of the body in pure water, while *wudhu* is a cleansing of certain parts of the body. *Ghusl* is done to purify major impurities, for example, after sexual relations. *Wudhu* is done to purify minor impurities. For each, the Muslim makes his intention to do so. Additionally, ablution helps us recover from our sins and bad habits.

Cleansing of the body helps rid toxins that are the root cause of most of the health problems. From the polluted air we breathe, the chemically laced food we eat, and the unfiltered water we drink, we are filled with toxins. As the skin is a prime candidate for toxins to enter, ablution to the skin areas can alleviate or remove toxins.

Ablution also protects us from eye infections and tooth decays, as we apply water both to our eyes and mouth. Ablution also helps rid unnecessary static electricity that we obtain from plastic products and atmospheric conditions. For example, washing the face helps reduce the amount of static electricity that could endanger the muscles under the skin resulting in wrinkles on our face.

Bear in mind that it is not just performing ablution once a day but multiple times a day to get the best results for our health. Ideally, if one performs ablution five times daily then the positive health effect is increased considerably.

Recitation

The importance of recitation in prayer is to concentrate and comprehend what is uttered. While reciting the verses about God's Blessings, we should seek His Help and Forgiveness. Prayer is the ideal time to recite verses from the Qur'an, as recitation helps bring us closer to God. Recitation should be done slowly with proper pronunciation.

The benefits of prayer recitation are that we fulfill God's Commandment as well as to keep Satan away. When we recite verses from the Qur'an, it should be done with full determination to adapt our life to the commands written in the Qur'an. In addition, as we are reciting verses from the Qur'an, we do so also to seek guidance to help us improve our lifestyles to be in conformity with Islam.

Reciting verses from the Qur'an during prayer is more excellent than reciting it at other times. Recitation should be done so as to make it pleasing to the ear and inspirational to the heart. As such, this will help the one praying contemplate the divine quality of the Qur'an.

During prayer recitation, the sounds of the words recited stimulate all organs of the body. As one is reciting, the overall physical structure of the body comes into harmony with itself, as posture is improved, mind is strengthened, vision is sharpened, and overall concentration is extended. Recitation gives us a sense of relaxation. It generates profound feelings of humility, modesty, and piety.

Prostration

"For Him (alone) is prayer in Truth: ...for the prayer of those without Faith is nothing but (futile) wandering (in the mind). Whatever beings there are in the Heavens and the Earth do prostrate themselves to God...." (Qur'an 13:14-15)

Prostration heightens our awareness, love, and remembrance of God, as we bow and kneel to Him in submission, obedience, humility, adoration, and honor. Prostration in prayer cannot be comprised or avoided unless, for example, the person is bedridden, disabled, incapacitated, in a battlefield, lost at sea, or escaping from a natural disaster such as an earthquake or volcanic eruption. As such, prostration is more than a physical attribute; it is spiritual and divinely mandated.

Prostration is a form of movement (kinetic energy) and is dependent on storage and release of the body's mechanical energy to be able to bend, kneel, and rise. During bending, kneeling, prostrating, and rising, the physical movements strengthen the joints and muscles as well as stimulate blood circulation. Like electricity, prayer is a form of energy. Like electrons or positive charged particles, uttering the words in a prayer elicits an electric current that flows through the entire body.

Each day, our bodies our adversely affected by electromagnetic waves emanating from lights and electrical products, such as appliances, televisions, cellular phones, computers, and motor vehicles. Prayer helps us discharge these electromagnetic waves that are harmful to our bodies. Muslims repeatedly prostrate throughout their five daily prayers. This act of prostration entails placing the forehead on the prayer rug. As a result, by placing the forehead on the surface and with deep concentration in prayer, harmful electromagnetic charges are discharged.

As we prostrate, we are humbling ourselves before God. It shows our appreciation, respect, and gratitude to Him. By prostrating, we rid ourselves of negative thoughts, such as greed, pride, and arrogance, so we can purify and enrich our souls as well as grow in wisdom.

Prostration purifies negative energy, as we raise our arms, bend and touch our knees, kneel and place our forehead on the prayer rug with our arms stretched out, rise up, and repeat the process again. This affords us the opportunity to energize our arms and legs, in fact, our entire body. Prostration has positive effects upon the back muscles, as they actively contract and become stronger. Even the neck muscles become stronger, as they bear the load when the forehead lies at the ground. In prostration, the whole body is in active motion (kinetic energy). When we place our forehead on the prayer rug, it is as if the gravity is pulling us towards the center of the Earth in the direction of the Holy Ka'bah in Mecca.

The effect of prayer works much like an electric generator, i.e., it converts energy into electrical current. This electric current can be envisioned as a form of fuel that energizes the body and mind. The end result is one of inspiration, as the mind conjures up positive thoughts and ideas.

The brain, an electrochemical organ, consists of matter and energy. Prayer is a way our brain manages and directs the energy force to cause real change in our own life situations. During prostration, the brain is now lower than the heart resulting in the blood streaming towards the brain with full force. This allows the brain to be nourished, which in turn greatly enhances our senses and ability to be more focused. Contrariwise, when not prostrating, the brain is above the heart, which has to work against gravity to send blood to the brain. Prayer is a force of energy as powerful as lightning, as it receives and sends electricity over long distances.

Prayer is focused energy, and its power connects us to the Creator. It stimulates the power of creative energy. Prayer is mental energy, emotional energy, and concentrated electrical energy that interconnects us with God. Prayer allows for the energy of healing. It is spiritual energy inspired by concentrated thought. As thought forms emerge, energy multiplies. The more faith and trust one has, the faster thought manifests into physical reality.

Through prayer, we learn to treat life with respect and responsibility. It is vibration energy producing high frequencies. Mechanical energy is utilized, as we perform our ablution and prostrate in prayer. As prayer is also a form of exercise, it is driven by mechanical energy, which helps strengthen the muscles in our body. Prayer can affect bodily chemicals (chemical energy) and reduce stress. Prayer improves respiratory efficiency and blood circulation. Prayer allows us to withstand the daily pressures and interruptions of life.

In preparation for our prayer, we may be in two types of energy – positive energy or negative energy. To pray is expressing strength within the body for it is creating a force within your emotional and physical reality to project the energy form as being positive or negative and experiencing it.

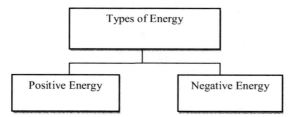

Positive Energy

Radiating positive energy to others as well as oneself is important. Prayer or meditation is the ideal way to raise the level of positive energy. With positive energy, we can clear our negative thoughts. Prayer boosts one's positive energy in manifold ways, such as erasing a bad memory or coping with an unfortunate incident. However, for positive energy to work, one's prayer must be sincere, honest, and passionate. Prayer is a form of meditation, which is the way we build the bridge between our conscious physical mind and our subconscious spiritual mind. By making this connection stronger each time we pray, we are establishing a permanent bridge between each of these minds.

We begin the day by making our intention to pray. This intention puts us in the proper frame of mind. It sets up a shield of protection during our spiritual prayers and also protects us throughout the day. This shield allows us to elicit positive energy to bring about a more concentrated prayer as well as to safeguard against performing anything bad. Excitement can create positive energies. For example, if we start our day with a positive insight, then we set up a pattern to react to situations, even bad situations, in a positive manner. The total time in performing the five daily prayers, including ablution, is about one hour. Focus on pulling this heightened spiritual awareness into our physical being, i.e., our conscious and subconscious minds.

If negative energy enters our life, we can start our morning introspection with a quick visualized scenario of clearing negative thoughts and energies from our mind. Then we can set the foundation of positive energy for the day. While we awaken in the morning and perform our intention to pray, we need to also state our intention to ward off evil thoughts before we sleep at night. There are many reasons why we would want to protect our energies. For example, we may want to set-up a force field around us each morning when we rise, which will sustain us until the evening. Of course, that force field begins with the Morning Prayer.

While praying, we need to exercise our lungs by taking deep breaths, which will help us relax thereby improving our level of concentration. With each exhale, envision all the stress, anxiety, and negativity we have leaving our body. With each inhale, picture the light collecting at our solar plexus (mass of nerve cells in the upper abdomen behind the stomach, kidneys, and other internal organs) beginning to enlarge. Imagine the warmth of the spiritual energy, as it passes through our muscles and organs. Imagine our entire body filled by this spiritual light, from the inside out.

Negative Energy

Negative emotions are extremely powerful. They can incapacitate lives very quickly by causing disparity in the energy system. This sets off a chain of emotional imbalance such as frustration, agony, mental instability, uncontrolled anger, inferiority complex, fear, and anxiety. Emotional imbalances, such as fear and anxiety, create negative energies that eventually culminate in illness.

If we start our day with a negative feeling, then we set up a pattern to react to situations in a negative way. Negative thoughts create negative energies, which establish negative activities or situations thereby creating negative thoughts again. Interacting with people with personal problems can drain our own energies; however, it is a charitable Islamic obligation to practice empathy and help those in need to overcome their troubles. However, when praying, it is preferred and highly recommended to be focused and not allow negative aspects from the bad people be an impediment to our concentration in prayer. But if we start our day with a little ritual of protection, i.e., intention, then negative people will not have an effect on us.

As negative energy accumulates, its gravitational pull causes us to engage in negative thoughts and feelings. This gravitational pull also attracts more negative energy from our surroundings, which intensifies the force. We need to understand how negative energy affects us, so we can seek a solution to remedy the problem. If we don't seek a solution, then negative energy will continue to affect our subconscious mind to the point that it overtakes our thoughts and feelings.

It would be difficult to remove obsessive thoughts from our conscious mind. We begin to experience erratic behavior that can have a devastating effect on our behavioral patterns both with ourselves and our surrounding environment. If the gravitational force escalates beyond the threshold point, then the negative thoughts and feelings might overpower our conscious mind and prevent us from enjoying life. We may become despondent, depressed, or withdrawn. As the intensity of negative energy builds, we begin to look for an escape mechanism. Escape is not the solution; it only gets worse. Our prayers are severely impacted, because we lose concentration and our thoughts begin to drift.

What we need is to learn how to protect and free ourselves in order to build an effective defense mechanism. The following is a plan of action:

- Increase the intensity of prayer and meditation (supplication) so as to help us from engaging in negative thoughts and feelings.

- Prayer and meditation help us focus our attention inside ourselves rather than on the outside world.

- Become habitual in reciting verses from the Qur'an, performing supplication, and asking for God's Blessing and Guidance in order to remove the negative energy that is already stored in our personal energy field.

- By creating a protective shield around our energy field, we can distance ourselves from engaging in problem areas that might have a negative impact on our thoughts and feelings.

We can use our mind power to transcend problems. When we link the negatives of the pain and suffering we encounter to the positives of success and happiness we derive, we create an energy that gives us the power to achieve even more success and happiness. The most effective process for doing this is prayer and meditation. Toward this end, we need to raise our own energy level, so it transforms any external negative energy into positive energy. Negative energy can only cling to negative energy. Positive energy repels it. Other people's negative energy can seep into us because we are not immune to it.

We are capable of both positive energy and negative energy, i.e., of sharing light and darkness. Our behavior, be it positive or negative, can deeply transform the behavior of others. Prayer and meditation transform not only the person who prays but the larger community as well. In prayer, the electric current is mindfulness and concentration. If we are mindful of our prayer, then we have concentration. We begin our prayer by being mindful of our gratitude to God, as we seek His Mercy and Forgiveness. The power of prayer is from within, and that power is patience and faith.

Congregational prayer further heightens one's positive energy. The congregation comes together to pray collectively. Praying together can be done in a mosque, the home, or at some other place. For example, the Friday Prayer at the mosque is performed by the collective participation of Muslims, as this is mandated in the Qur'an. Congregational prayer is so important that Muslims even observe it at the most dangerous times, e.g., in the battlefield during war. This coming together in prayer is the best prescription for purifying one's body, mind, and soul. In fact, this purification during the congregational prayer is a better form of exercise than that offered by fitness centers. Even the brain becomes more clear and focused, and the physical nature of one's body improves significantly.

During congregational prayer, the body expends energy. Normally, the human body perspires to keep our bodies from overheating. Perspiration energizes the body. Perspiration is like a fire department in that it brings the heat temperature down to a safe level. By cooling the body, perspiration allows more energy to be burned. This energizing allows one to feel better and become more focused in meditation. Additionally, congregational prayer and perspiration may enable the person to be less dependent on medication, as the body detoxes ridding our system of toxic substances and bodily wastes. Even during the Hajj (Pilgrimage), perspiration cools the body from the intense heat, as large groups of Muslims are making their circumambulation around the Ka'bah in Mecca.

Prostration and Energy of the Sun

The Sun is the source of most of the energy on Earth. If it were not for the Sun, the Earth would be a cold, lifeless world. According to many scientists, the Sun is about 4.5 billion years old, and that it will begin to die in about 5 billion years. As the Sun grows old, it will expand, and then cool, become less bright, and shrink. Scientists further theorize that the Sun is in a state of constant loss of energy, and that it will ultimately die as a star, implode, and absorb the Earth into its supra-dense mass:

"And the Sun travelled unto a resting-place fixed for it; that is the decree of the All-Mighty, the All-Knowing." (Qur'an 36:38)

The *resting-place* in this verse is the translation of the Arabic word **mustaqarr.** Each day, the Sun prostrates, rests, and then rises again the next day. Just as we ask God for permission to rise from our state of prostration, the Sun also asks God for permission to rise from its state of prostration. Likewise, all the Heavenly bodies ask God for permission to arise from their prostration, for example, the moon and stars that light the sky at night. While the Arabic word **sujood** means prostration or bowing down to God as a necessary act during prayer, it also means complete obedience to God. As with mankind, the Heavenly bodies must be in complete obedience to God:

"...and the sun and the moon and the stars, made (absolutely) subservient to His Command...." (Qur'an 7:54)

When the "Final Hour" arrives, those who were negligent in prayer cannot turn back the clock realizing that they should have prostrated in prayer. Our energy as well as all the energy of the Heavenly bodies will eventually come to an end:

"What! Wait they then for aught save the Hour (of Reckoning) that it come on them all of a sudden? Indeed have (already) come the signs of it; and of what avail can be the reminder to them when it hath already come on them?" (Qur'an 47:18)

Fasting

Fasting *(siyam)* is referred to as self-restraint:

"O you who believe! Fasting is prescribed to you as it was prescribed to those before you, that you may (learn) self-restraint." (Qur'an 2:183)

"Ramadan is the (month) in which was sent down the Qur'an, as a guide to mankind, also clear (signs) for guidance and judgment (between right and wrong). So every one of you who is present (at his home) during that month should spend it in fasting...." (Qur'an 2:185)

During fasting, Muslims abstain primarily from eating, drinking, smoking, and sex from dawn to dusk. Ramadan, according to Prophet Mohammad, is:

"...a month of endurance (sabr), and the reward for endurance is Paradise...a month in which a believer's provisions are increased."[40]

Ramadan

It is incumbent upon Muslims to fast during the month of Ramadan, the ninth month of the Islamic lunar calendar. Muslims, for example, who are traveling, sick, or frail due to old age, may be exempt from fasting.

While travelling may exempt a person from fasting, those whose occupation necessitates that they travel should fast. While those who are exempt from fasting due to their medical condition, fasting can help or even cure some diseases. Fasting allows Muslims to heal themselves. Those afflicted with certain diseases, such as gastrointestinal disorders, can benefit from fasting. Fasting cleanses our bodies and can greatly help in addressing weight problems and diabetes. Nonetheless, missed fasts must be done at another time when the Muslim completes his travel or restores his health. There are penalties for violating an obligatory fast. The type of violation will determine the extent of the penalty.

There are other recommended fasts outside the month of Ramadan, such as the fast during the first and third days of the month Muharram, the months of Rajab and Sha'ban, and the first and last Thursday of every lunar month, just to mention a few. One of the ways to practice self-restraint during the month of Ramadan is to recite the entire Qur'an during that month. All Muslims, rich and poor, come into balance during Ramadan, as all are equally engaging in the same type of abstention. During this month, the Muslim becomes healthier due to a balance in the diet, a more balanced character due to self-restraint, and a reward from God for abstention and submission.

Fasting self actualizes us in self-restraint, so that we can practice patience, self-control, and self-discipline. Our consciousness is heightened during fasting, as we become more responsible and accountable for our actions. Our ultimate aim in fasting is to strive towards the purification of the soul.

Stored Energy Sources

The body's energy sources are displayed in the following diagram:

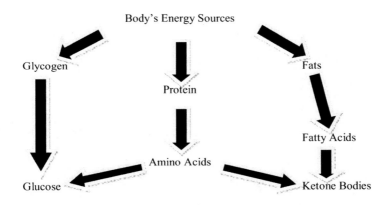

Blood glucose levels must be maintained by the breakdown of stored energy (glycogen and amino acid breakdown). Carbohydrates are broken down into simple sugars, e.g., glucose. Proteins are broken down into amino acids. Fats are broken down into fatty acids. Released free fatty acids are taken up by the liver and metabolized for energy. When there are large amounts of free fatty acids released, they are broken down and released into the blood as ketone bodies to provide another source of energy for cells. Amino acids, released from protein breakdown are used by the liver. The brain uses blood glucose as its energy source.[41]

The principle of fasting is simple. When the intake of food is temporarily stopped, many systems of the body are given a break from the hard work of digestion. The extra energy gives the body the chance to heal and restore itself, and burning stored calories gets rid of toxic substances stored in the body. Fats and carbohydrates are stored (potential energy) of which the body burns off chemical energy. Chemically, a fast begins when the body's carbohydrate stores begin to be used as an energy source. The fast will continue, as long as fat and carbohydrate stores are used for energy.

Muslims fast during the entire month of Ramadan, beginning their fast at dawn and ending their fast at dusk. During fasting, food and water intake are stopped. In the course of the daily fasting period, the body rests allowing the digestive tract to relax. At this time, much-

51

needed rest allows the body to heal itself, as stored calories are burned off and stored toxic substances disposed of. Fasting is not starvation but, rather, the body's burning of stored energy.

Ketosis

During fasting, once the body uses up sugars (its basic energy supply), it starts to consume fat. Dr. Shahid Athar states that food is needed by the body to produce energy for immediate use by utilizing carbohydrates, that is, sugar. An excess carbohydrate that cannot be used is stored up as fat tissue in muscles, and as glycogen in liver for future use. Insulin, a hormone from the pancreas, lowers blood sugar and diverts it to other forms of energy storage, that is, glycogen.

According to Dr. Athar, when one fasts, or decreases carbohydrate intake drastically, it lowers the blood glucose and insulin level. This causes a breakdown of glycogen from liver to provide glucose for energy needs and breakdown of fat from adipose tissue to provide for energy needs.

In order to save important muscle during a fast, a protein process called ketosis is energized. Ketosis occurs very early in the fasting period, usually around the second or third day of the fast. Ketosis is characterized by elevated levels of ketone bodies in the blood, occurring when the liver converts stored fat and other nonessential tissues into ketones. As an alternative to glucose, ketones can be used by the body for energy.

Ketones are a by-product or waste product when the body burns stored fat for energy. During a fast, a person is hungry; therefore, fat burns because glucose is unavailable. These ketones are essential to provide much-needed energy to the heart, brain, and muscles. As a result, sensations of hunger subside, and those who fast may experience normal or even increased levels of energy. However, if the body burns too much fat too quickly, ketones will accumulate in the bloodstream and make the body too acidic. This acidity will upset the body's chemical balance.[42]

Detoxification

Detoxification is the removal of toxic substances from the body. Kidneys and liver are the main detoxification organs, so detoxifying means to activate the detoxifying organs. Detoxification through the kidneys regulates the body's fluid volume, mineral composition, and acidity. Detoxification through the liver makes fat soluble homotoxins water soluble to excrete them over the kidneys and the bile. As the skin is the main channel over which toxins get into the body and intoxicate the organism, detoxification through the skin entails drainage or excretion of toxic substances. The main function of the colon is to excrete waste from the body, but it is also used in water absorption. The main mucosal membranes are the gastrointestinal and the intestinal. By activating defense cells, these mucosal membranes play a crucial role in the detoxification of the organism.[43]

Poor eating habits lead to toxic substances in the body. Because our bodies are continuously attacked with toxic substances, a good diet will help keep the body detoxified. While we are asleep, our body has a few hours to cleanse itself. When we awake in the morning, we can feel the effects of toxic acid, for example, foul breath. With poor eating habits, numerous toxins rapidly enter into the bloodstream.

In preparation for fasting, it helps to have a balanced diet at least two weeks prior to Ramadan. This diet consists of drinking plenty of water and eating fresh fruit and vegetables along with balanced meals.

Even during the month of Ramadan, we should avoid the fast-food diets that do not allow the body to cleanse itself of toxins. For example, when the intake of calories is greater than burned, the results will be stored body fat. It is the same with toxins. A meal of hamburgers, French fries, soft drinks, ice cream, and cake, will result in the intake of toxins to be greater than toxins that are removed. This toxic overload is prevalent among persons who are overweight or obese, as they are carriers of a storehouse of toxins that affect normal cell functions. When the toxic load is greater than what the body can handle, the person can become sick or weaken his immune system.

Fasting Benefits

The benefits of fasting are highlighted in Dr. Jack Goldstein's book, *Triumph over Disease by Fasting and Natural Diet.*[44] He says that the benefits for fasting are:

- to conserve the energies of the body so they may be diverted to whatever the body is trying to accomplish;

- to secure physiologic rest for vital organs, i.e., rest of the digestive, glandular, circulatory, respiratory, and nervous systems, as well as to repair damaged organs;

- to eliminate metabolic waste from the blood and tissues, so that toxics are thrown out and the system becomes purified thereby improving one's health;

- to stop the intake of foods that decompose in the intestines and further poison the body;

- to allow the body to adjust and normalize its biochemistry and also its secretions (glandular fluids);

- to let the body break down and absorb swellings, deposits, diseased tissues, and abnormal growths;

- to restore a youthful condition to the cells and tissues;

- to permit the conservation and re-routing of energy;

- to increase the powers of digestion and assimilation, i.e., absorption and utilization of food into the system; and

- to clear and strengthen the mind.

The foregoing presents a very convincing reason to fast. It should be noted that fasting does not deplete the blood, produce anemia, cause the heart to weaken or collapse, reduce resistance to disease, or cause mental disturbances. During the fast, the system of secretion is organized, and this in turn benefits the blood pressure, inhibiting hardening of the arteries.

Will Carroll states that due to the lack of incoming energy, the body must turn to its own resources, a function called autolysis. Autolysis is the breaking down of fat stores in the body in order to produce energy. Carroll further states that the benefit of fasting is the healing process that begins during a fast. During a fast, energy is diverted away from the digestive system due to its lack of use and towards the metabolism and immune system. During a fast, the healing process is precipitated by the body's search for energy sources.[45]

From the foregoing discussion, the following gives us a brief synopsis of the importance of fasting to our health:

- Burns off chemical energy from potential energy (carbohydrates and fats).

- Eliminates toxins that break down the body's immune system (detoxification).

- Eliminates all unusable waste and hardened material in joints and muscles.

- Cleanses the kidneys and digestive system.

- Natural healing and cleansing system that reaches each cell and tissue.

- Purifies the glands and cells throughout the body.

- Helps normalize weight, blood pressure, and cholesterol.

- Relieves pressure and irritation in nerves, arteries, and blood vessels.

- Breakfast digests foods from chemical energy (stored in nutrients) and converts them into mechanical energy (movement).

Because fasting entails long hours, we should consume slow-digesting foods, including fiber foods, rather than fast-digesting foods. Slow-digesting foods are complex carbohydrates, which include wheat, lentils, and grains. Fast-digesting foods are refined carbohydrates, which include sugar and white flour. Fiber foods include vegetables and dried fruits. Meat, chicken, fish, and dairy products should be added to bring about a balanced diet. It is vital to drink plenty of water and liquids. We should avoid fried foods and fatty foods.

The human energy system is strengthened with fasting. Fasting is both therapeutic and spiritual, which allows energetic cleansing of the body and mind to bring them into balance and harmony with each other. As a result, Muslims become more attuned to not only their health needs but also to those with whom they come in contact with. By fasting, concentration, confidence, self-esteem, and self-control are improved considerably, as Muslims become more attentive and responsive to their Islamic duties and obligations.

For Muslims, the balanced energy derived from fasting results into a better quality of life:

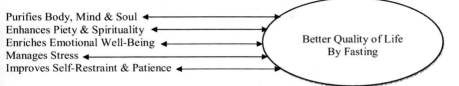

Purifies Body, Mind & Soul
Enhances Piety & Spirituality
Enriches Emotional Well-Being
Manages Stress
Improves Self-Restraint & Patience

Better Quality of Life
By Fasting

Fasting is an expression of wholeheartedness and puts things in proper perspective. As fasting purifies our body, mind, and soul, it helps express, deepen, and confirm our gratitude to God. Fasting gives us the opportunity to enhance our piety and spirituality so that we can become better Muslims. We fast to demonstrate our love and remembrance of God. Toward this end, fasting enriches our emotional and intellectual well-being. Stress has been a silent killer and difficult to cope with. However, fasting is the remedy to manage stress and improve our daily lives. During fasting, it is self-restraint and patience that helps us endure the month of Ramadan.

ENERGY HEALTH IN ISLAM

SPIRITUAL

PHYSICAL

EMOTIONAL

MENTAL

CHAPTER 4

ENERGY TRANSFORMATION

In order to have a healthy body and mind, we need to bring into balance food and nutrition, fitness and exercise, and relaxation and stress management. With a positive attitude, we can motivate ourselves to improve our overall health and well-being. We are constantly seeking better ways to improve our health and lifestyle. Oftentimes, we are neglectful and abuse our bodies resulting in severe health problems. We seek a physician's help who, for the most part, treats the symptom but not the cause. Overwhelmed with the fast pace of society and its problematic issues, we become affected either physically, emotionally, mentally, or spiritually:

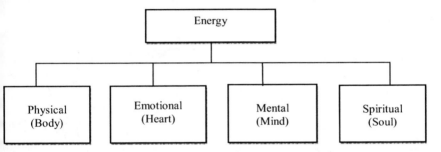

The energy fields of physical (body), emotional (heart), mental (mind), and spiritual (soul) can have an effect on our entire body's health system. To underscore the impact that these can have on our well-being, let us just look at how emotions can have a profound effect on our physical body. Constant stress affects our hormones and our nervous system, which can contribute to the development of ulcers, heart disease, and a host of other illnesses.

Restructuring the sluggish areas of our mental and emotional levels of energy can help remove emotional blocks. Additionally, this restructuring may also allow energy to flow in these sluggish areas and help us grasp the fundamental issues of our illness. Trauma is such an illness, which can appear in or energy field, and this traumatic distortion can affect not only our physical body but also our emotions, mental state of mind, and spiritual well-being. The end result can be a painful experience and lead to a more advanced form of disease.

What is needed is a reconnect to improve our health situation, and that reconnect is Islam. Some of the reasons we seek this Islamic health reconnect are:

- Physical sickness, surgery, disability

- Emotional despondency, hopelessness, sadness

- Mental lapse, disorientation, depression

- Spiritual decline, disenchantment, distrust

These health issues require immediate attention. Help is needed. Something is wrong. We can turn to Islam and its benefits to reconnect and energize our health. The following displays how Islam transforms, reconnects, and energizes health to bring about our overall well-being:

Energy Transformation
Islamic Health Reconnect

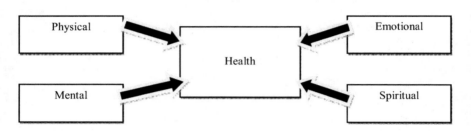

The benefits derived from an Islamic reconnect are manifold. Some of these are:

- Alleviates physical pain from trauma (praying)

- Eliminates metabolic wastes in body (fasting)

- Enriches emotional well-being (praying)

- Manages stress (fasting)

- Heightens mental awareness (praying)

- Enhances piety and spirituality (fasting)

Today, we notice people spending considerable time purchasing a house or car, rather than discussing their health concerns with a physician. However, physicians have a tendency to spend more time writing prescriptions than they do trying to find the cause of an ailment. Just trace back how many times we went to a physician for a physical ailment, and often their immediate solution is let's wait and see if the matter can be resolved with drugs or whether it gets worse. This leaves our emotional, mental, and spiritual conditions still in disarray. Physicians may treat a physical wound, but they usually do not address the mental, emotional, and spiritual aspects, all of which are important to our well-being. This means that we need to seek alternative ways to heal not just the physical body but also the mental, emotional, and spiritual aspects as well.

Physical Energy

Energy flows through our spinal cords and nervous systems as electrical impulses. Many people are comfortable about their bodies; however, they have limited knowledge as to how their bodies function. Why? We touch and feel our skin and we feel comfortable. We bathe our bodies and we feel refreshed. We may not understand how the skin functions, or if we didn't bathe what would happen to our bodies, for example, skin disorders, odor, fungus, etc.

The physical body contains organs, systems, brain, mind, emotions, and a soul. A chemical system with the occurrence of many chemical reactions is located within our physical body. Chemical reactions interact with nerves, muscles, tissues, and cells within our body. At times, we wonder why we have a craving for a certain food, even though we know that food is detrimental to our health. Yet, we continue to eat that food and don't know why. What we don't understand is that it is our body that is asking for that particular food. In other words, the craving is activated by a chemical reaction.

Even the medical profession has limited knowledge as to how the body functions, although it has come a long way with technological advancements and research. True, our knowledge about how to heal a broken bone has advanced considerably; however, how to cure cancer is still in the distant future. Still more perplexing is how the physical body responds to different emotions and thoughts. A snapshot of physical energy is as follows:

- Fundamental source of fuel

- Affects our ability to manage all of the other energies

- Depends on:
  - Patterns of movement and breathing
  - Foods we eat
  - Rest and recovery

Emotional Energy

The chemical reactions in our bodies change depending on which types of emotions we are feeling. Let us look at the example of one being happy versus being angry, and how the chemical reactions impact the physical body. When one feels happy, chemical reactions allow the body to become relaxed. This relaxation can be an inducement for that person to restore his or her health. However, when someone is angry, chemical reactions will create stress on various organs in the body. This stress results in the person becoming very uneasy, and if the stress continues it can have a negative impact on the person's body, for example, the heart. Should this emotional stress persist, then the possibility of a heart attack can occur.

What is disturbing is that medicine treats the body, as if emotions have no effect. If arteries in our bodies are clogged, then a physician proceeds to unclog the arteries. The patient may be put on a strict diet, so the arteries are prevented from clogging again. But the physician didn't take into account that an emotional imbalance may also have contributed to the clogged arteries and, as such, no recommendation was made in this regard.

We know little about how to deal and live with our emotions or feelings. Emotions that are ignored remain in our bodies, i.e., in our organs, muscles, and overall physical body system. Releasing these emotions necessitate chemical reactions. Happiness and love elicit certain chemical reactions, while hate and fear elicit other chemical reactions. A snapshot of emotional energy is as follows:

- Capacity to manage emotions:
  - High positive energy
  - Full engagement
  - Peak performance
- Key factors:
  - Self-Confidence & Self-Control
  - Social Skills & Enjoyment
  - Empathy & Openness
  - Patience & Trust

Emotional Intelligence and Creative Energy

Emotional intelligence can be defined in terms of self-awareness, altruism, personal motivation, empathy, and the ability to love and be loved by friends, partners, and family members. It is a type of social intelligence that involves the ability to monitor each other's emotions, to discriminate among them, and to use the information to guide our thinking and actions. People with high emotional intelligence skills get along better and don't let anxieties and frustrations get in the way of efficiently solving problems. It increases the understanding between people, which minimizes time wasted arguing and being defensive. It is the ability to sense, understand, and effectively apply the power of emotions, appropriately channeled as a source of human energy, creativity, and influence. Emotions are the primary source of human energy, aspiration, authenticity, and drive, activating our innermost feelings and purpose in life, and transforming them from things we think about, to values we live.[46] The heart is the place of courage and spirit, integrity, and commitment – the source of energy and deep feelings that call us to create, learn, cooperate, lead, and serve. When we have painful feelings, the heart is telling us we have unmet needs, or we are interpreting reality through some kind of distorting filter. When we have positive feelings, the heart is telling us we are pointing in the right direction, towards fulfillment of our needs and towards truth. Emotions move energy and bring things into motion, or manifestation. The force behind what we feel is what allows us to create. First we have our thought, or perception. But it is the emotional energy, the fuel that allows something to get created.[47]

Creative energy transforms our thoughts and feelings by empowering and inspiring us to make positive changes in our lives. As such, creative energy is internally released from within us and channeled to the external environment as an expression of who we are or what we want to do. The dynamic nature of creative energy demands release; it must be expressed. For example, as the artist paints a picture, he channels his creative energy by releasing his thoughts and feelings. This release is a form of emotional expression as well as his motivation of how he feels it will be interpreted by his viewers. The viewers, in turn, channel their creative energy in the form of expression, as to how they actually interpret the art work. Creative energy fosters a sense of inner security and confidence that allows one to experiment with new ideas. These experiences are realized, once our emotions are motivated and ready to act. Like a stream of consciousness, expression can release creative energy and free the person to be more lively, vibrant, and spontaneous. To become directly aware of the creative energy, however, we must steer our perception outside consciousness itself. To think creatively, one must break through repressed energy barriers and begin to experience a larger energy field.

Mental Energy

The central nervous system in our bodies executes commands either automatically or through the mind. While the heart functions independently of the mind, a person may picture in his mind dreadful consequences, and this will increase the beating of the heart. Similarly, when one prays or meditates, the beating of the heart will slow down. The mind thinks, reasons, perceives, and wills.

Walter Russell's book entitled, *The Message of the Divine Iliad*, states that man's actions are a direct result of his thinking. Human beings manufacture their own physical and mental agony by unbalanced decisions and actions regarding personal, business and social relations. Our brains are electric storehouses for memories recorded upon them, as a result of the experiences of our senses. The brain is the nerve center of all parts of the body, which motivates the body to perform various functions. The brain of man is not his mind. The mind is cosmic. Our behavioral patterns are influenced by our thought processes.[48] Therefore, if we change the way we think, then we can change the way we behave. Our beliefs and value systems have evolved over time, and they have become part of our mental state of mind. A snapshot of mental energy is as follows:

- Regulates flow of fuel to the brain

- Capacity to sustain concentration and focus:

    - Prayer, Fasting & Pilgrimage

- Maintain optimistic perspective:

    - Charity

- Mental preparation:

    - Jihad (Struggle)

Spiritual Energy

Energetic health on a spiritual level can close the gap between whom we are and who we aspire to be. In the spiritual sense, there is a greater purpose in life. We see the creation everywhere, and we marvel at the wonders of this creation. We know a greater force exists that connects everything together.

The common denominator in the Universe is energy. We are energetic beings, and it is the spiritual aspect of energy that reinforces the physical, mental, and emotional aspects of our health. If we lack worship, then our health is adversely impacted. For our body and mind to be healthy, we need to lead a life of spirituality. Spiritual values need to be integrated into our lifestyles. We are surrounded by an electromagnetic energy field, which contain unseen patterns of energy that influence the way we think and act. The power of prayer and meditation brings all the energy forces of physical, emotional, mental, and spiritual in harmony with each other. A snapshot of spiritual energy is as follows:

- Creative energy, mediation, consciousness & transcendence

- Enlightenment, energy healing & self-realization

- Brings mind and senses under control

- Brings body and mind into balance

- Activates and self-actualizes patience/endurance (*sabr*)

Human Energy Field

The human energy field is the structure upon which the cells of the body grow. Not only is it the foundation for the body but also the connectivity between body and mind. Therefore, the human energy field is directly connected with health and illness. As the human energy field sets the foundation for the body, anything that goes wrong with it will ultimately impact the body. There is a direct correlation between the human energy field and the thought patterns that emerge from our brain. For example, any expressions or feelings that we elicit will generate energy. As we change our thought patterns, the pattern of the human energy field also changes. Even the Muslim concept of intention emerges from a deeper level of the human energy field. Intention is a learned process that directly affects the human energy field and, therefore, strongly affects our health. The Qur'an states:

"...Verily never will God change the condition of a people until they change it themselves (with their own souls)." (Qur'an 13:11)

God gave man the intelligence and knowledge to change the condition to improve their well-being. How people change is by generating positive energy to be obedient to God and to seek the unity in Islam. The nature of change must come from within us. If we remain on the

63

straight path, our good condition will remain. However, if we stray from the straight path, unless we repent to God, our condition will not be changed. In order to return to the straight path, we need to make our intention to change so God can fulfill our request for change. This change elicits positive energy so we can maintain a healthy energy field.

We all desire to be healthy. As such, we need to create and maintain balance on all energetic levels to stay healthy. When energetic imbalance occurs and symptoms arise, we know that medicine can help the symptoms but that energetic blockages can still exist, unless we investigate the root cause of the ailment. Restoring the energetic health flow on all levels, by releasing energetic blockages, brings about balance in the total system. Awareness of how we feel and think is a step toward restoring a healthy system.

We need to redirect ourselves toward wanting to be healthy in order to reconnect our human energy field in a positive and lasting process. We need to adapt our own human energy field in order to repair, clear, and move it toward greater health. This shift in the energy patterns can in turn manifest as physical health, as well as improved emotional, mental and spiritual health. The following is a compendium of the human energy field, as it applies to the four levels of energy: physical, emotional, mental, and spiritual:

Physical Energy:

- Explores the environment and the laws of nature by way of the senses.

- Directs the movement of organs and bodily functions toward health attainment.

Emotional Energy:

- Shapes the Islamic personality and interaction with others.

- Irregular fluctuations associated with various levels of feelings that usually interact with physical energy.

Mental Energy:

- Consists of beliefs and practical applications associated with various thought patterns.

- Degree of reaction to thoughts closely aligned with emotional energy.

Spiritual Energy:

- Reflects awareness of what is learned and experienced.

- Probes mental energy and conscience energy to self-actualize in faith, righteous deeds, truth, and patience.

Why is it important to have balance in our human energy field? The reason is that our human energy field influences our lives. When our human energy field is out of balance, it means that there are distortions and distractions impairing our judgments both in the way we think and in the way we feel and act. As we disconnect from the energy balance of physical, emotional, mental, and spiritual, we lose connectivity with ourselves and the environment in which we live. In effect, we lose consciousness of our purpose in life.

The human energy field continuously interacts with the environmental energy field. As we evolve toward the meaning and purpose of our existence, we are constantly organizing ourselves in the changing and complex environment. This self-organization provides us with an identity that is molded by our interaction with the environmental energy field. How we influence change is through our intention and ability to choose, which gives meaning to our self-identity. It is this awareness that has a direct impact on our human energy field.

Our dynamic environment undergoes a continuous transformation of energy with matter and information. Transformation is the direct result of the interaction of our human energy field with the environmental energy field. How we bring into balance our human energy field with the environmental energy field enhances our well-being and overall health.

What is needed to bring about this balance is therapy, and the best therapy is prayer. Just a short Morning Prayer, for example, of less than five minutes can bring this balance about on all four planes: physical, emotional, mental, and spiritual. In effect, this balance brings about unity within our bodies and minds. In turn, this unity transcends all levels of existence, i.e., nature, our environment, and those with whom we come in contact with.

Islamic Healing

Shaykh Hisham Muhammad Kabbani, an Islamic scholar as well as a medical doctor, has since the 1990s pursued interfaith dialogue in America by meeting with and lecturing on the faith of Islam to leaders and congregations of other faiths. His knowledge about Islam and medicine qualifies him to speak on the subject of Islamic healing. In his *Spiritual Healing in the Islamic Tradition*, he gives us a prescription to bring about harmony and balance within our energy field. He states that through the meditative process of spiritual healing, one can access this driving energy that exists in every living cell of the body. Shaykh Kabbani postulates that a positive energy flow nourishes the non-physical body and maintains its structure and foundation, balancing the human system. This balance leads to increased awareness of the body's sensations that in turn leads to good living, following a proper diet, and enjoyment of exercise. The non-physical body then supports and maintains a healthy physical body, in which the chemical and physical systems remain balanced and functioning normally, thus perpetuating physical health.

In the healthy system, the energies in each body not only remain balanced but also support and influence the energy balance in other people's bodies. Meditation is a tool that gives deep relaxation and quiets the mind. Meditation also helps alleviate stress and enable the internal chemical and hormonal system to regain their equilibrium.[49] While Shaykh Kabbani asserts that positive energy has a major impact on the human system, it is the intention that surfaces from the human energy field that drives the positive energy. Intention directly affects our health through the human energy field.

The Qur'an refers to the structure of thermal energy and the concept of vibrating weaved ropes in the following verses:

"By the sky with its numerous paths (weaved ropes)." (Qur'an 51:7)

"Do not the unbelievers see that the Heavens and the Earth were joined together (as one unit of creation), before we clove them asunder? We made from water every living thing. Will they not then believe?" (Qur'an 21:30)

"And among His (God) signs in this: thou seest the Earth barren and desolate; but when we send down rain to it, it is stirred (vibrates) to life and yields increase (grows)...." (Qur'an 41:39)

"And God made you grow of the Earth as a growth (of a plant)." (Qur'an 71:17)

According to the Qur'an, the propagation of all forms of energy needs to be exactly like the propagation of energy in water. In other words, living creatures are made of matter through which energy propagates to maintain the various functions of the living creatures. Therefore, we can conclude from the Qur'an that the energy in God's creation is composed of weaved ropes vibrating at certain frequencies. How vibrating weaved ropes impact matter and energy can be summarized in the following:

- Thermal energy is transmitted as electromagnetic radiation like light waves.

- Color of matter changes with increased heating:

  - Color of metal changes from red to blue with increased heating.

- Sun is a source of thermal energy.

- Thermal energy produced from the sun is composed of vibrating energy weaved ropes.

- God's creation is composed of weaved ropes vibrating at certain frequencies.

- Matter is composed of weaved fabric of atoms.

- Interaction of energy weaved ropes with matter:

  - When rain falls on the Earth, it vibrates and grows bringing forth plants and trees.

  - God made every living thing from water, which propagates as droplets of matter that contains a certain amount of vibrating energy.

Even the source of growth energy for plants and trees emanates from the Earth, which is gravitational energy in the shape of weaved ropes. Dr. Zaid Ghazzawi, in his book, *The Law of Everything as Derived from the Noble Qur'an*, discusses the concept of *thermal energy and weaved ropes* in Islam. With a mechanical engineering background and a doctorate in biomedical engineering from the University of Surrey in England, Dr. Ghazzawi has given numerous lectures on the topic of miracles of knowledge in the Qur''an. He believes that the vibratory state of gravitational energy must come from the vibrations of the basic building blocks of the gravitational field that are weaved ropes. These ropes are not static but are in a dynamical vibratory state. The vibrations of these ropes are exactly like the flow of water waves such that each rope vibrates in exactly a similar manner to the vibrations of water droplets in a water wave. That energy waves for all forms of energy in God's creation follow the same mechanics as does the interaction of water waves. God teaches us that the Heavens contain weaved ropes, and that the function of weaved ropes is to produce a pulling action between the objects they are linked to. Therefore, it can be concluded that energy exhibits the behavior of both waves and energy particles.

Dr. Ghazzawi further states that the amount of energy experienced by a materialistic object is mainly proportional to the density of energy weaved ropes the object is experiencing, i.e., the number of ropes divided by the volume the ropes cover. The density of these ropes is in turn proportional to the proximity of the object to the source of energy. As the object gets closer to the source of energy, the more energy ropes are experienced by the object (higher energy), and as the object moves further from the source of energy, the density of energy weaved ropes decreases (lower energy).[50]

In support of Dr. Ghazzawi's theory that weaved ropes generate vibrating energy, if we look at the atoms within our physical bodies, we can find patterns of vibrating energy that we have called matter. Our physical bodies are really fields of vibrating energies. As there are various fields of vibrating energies, then one field can impact or interact with another field. For example, there are vibrating energies for each of our body's organs or each cell within our body. These vibrating energies determine whether or not our organs and cells are healthy or unhealthy.

Our emotional state is affected by vibrating energies that shape our personality and whether we are, for example, happy or sad. Our mental and spiritual levels are affected by vibrating energies, in that our conscience impacts the way we act and the way we think and feel. Through the vehicles of prayer and fasting, Muslims are able to harmonize these weaved vibrating energies into a balanced state of energy that is physical, emotional, mental, and spiritual.

Energy is movement and movement is vibration. All matter has a pattern of vibration and is infused with energy. All life in the Universe, including mankind, is animated by energy. We often hear sounds from the ringing of bells, toots of a horn, clapping of hands, or the falling rain. This sound is a form of energy. Our ears capture the audible frequency of sound waves via the vibrating air. The sound then passes from the inner ear to the brain through electrical nerve signals.

Energy Equilibrium and Islamic Well-Being

A balanced state of our body's system necessitates equilibrium of energy for the well-being of our health. This equilibrium is based on energy intake and energy output:

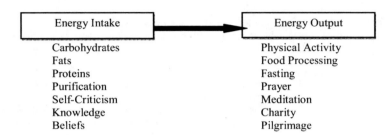

Energy Intake	Energy Output
Carbohydrates	Physical Activity
Fats	Food Processing
Proteins	Fasting
Purification	Prayer
Self-Criticism	Meditation
Knowledge	Charity
Beliefs	Pilgrimage

The definition of energy equilibrium is the balance between energy intake and energy output. Both energy intake and energy output are influenced by our physical, emotional, mental, spiritual aspects. Examples of energy intake are carbohydrates, fats, and proteins as well as purification, self-criticism, knowledge, and beliefs. Examples of energy output are physical activity, food processing, fasting, prayer, meditation, charity, and pilgrimage. Energy intake is also influenced by food and drink, while energy output is also influenced by genetics, body size, and amount of muscle.

From a physical aspect, it is not just a matter of calorie intake versus calorie output, even though calories are a critical element in maintaining energy balance. Other factors in our diet are also important, for example, the amount of fiber or calcium we eat may also influence our energy output as well as how much muscle and fat we have.

Our body uses fuel and expends energy for three primary purposes: (a) maintain basic physiological functions such as breathing and blood circulation; (c) to power physical activity; and (c) to process food we eat. The major components of energy output or energy expenditure are (a) resting energy expenditure, i.e., energy for basic body functions that are affected by body size, composition, age, and gender; (b) physical activity is highly variable and affected by body size, fitness level, and type of activity; and (c) thermal effect of food i.e., energy to digest, absorb, and metabolize food. Energy output helps control weight and improves health, mobility, and quality of life. In addition, energy output helps decrease morbidity, pain, and discomfort.

In Islam, moderation creates equilibrium, so that we are at peace with ourselves. It helps us avoid extremes in negative emotions or positive emotions, for example, extreme sadness that may depress us or extreme happiness that renders a false sense of celebration. It is for us to avoid extremes and to maintain balance and moderation, so that we may perform our functions properly. By bringing us in balance with ourselves, moderation heightens our awareness to be tolerant and just. Moderation encompasses all aspects of human conduct, both in personal matters and in social life. As such, moderation is the key for all moral and ethical principles and values of Islam.

Managing Energy

The many problems and pressures that we are confronted with have a considerable impact on our body and mind. The global economic downturn that escalated in the year 2009 has literally devastated families not only financially but physically, emotionally, mentally, and spiritually. Stress is endemic and in some communities pandemic. How to cope with ongoing issues in the society that have a detrimental effect on how we live is a major concern. What we need is to energize ourselves with highest performance possible. We need to better focus ourselves to cope with stress, and to be able to improve our level of concentration. In short, we need to be more productive within ourselves. We need to manage our energy.

Jim Loehr and Tony Schwartz, in the *Power of Full Engagement*, state that we need to rethink much of what we have believed about organizing our lives. They state that to be fully engaged in our lives, we must be physically energized, emotionally connected, mentally focused, and spiritually aligned with a purpose beyond our immediate self-interest. They further advise us that (a) energy is the fundamental currency of high performance; and (b) performance, health, and happiness are grounded in the skillful management of energy.[51]

Heidi Katz, in her *Managing Energy for Sustained High Performance*, builds upon the four principles of energy management proposed by Loehr and Schwartz:[52]

1. Energy has 4-dimensions: physical, mental, emotional, and spiritual. It is necessary to draw energy from each domain and to manage our energy in all four.

2. Energy is best managed when there is ebb and flow between stress and recovery. Stress in this context is meant in a positive sense. Stress results when we stretch ourselves and use our talents and skills beyond the expected; however, it must be balanced with recovery and rest, and most of us don't know how to do this. Without recovery and rest, work product suffers, mistakes are made, performance excellence is not possible – and, too, illness can result.

3. Pushing beyond our usual limits of course builds our strengths. Building mental, emotional, and spiritual capacities is similar to physical training to improve our physical strength. We must push in order to grow.

4. Creating specific positive energy-replenishing rituals sustains and expands our energy. This is the key to recuperating and making our energy reserves fully available to us.

Relative to the human psyche and its receptiveness to change physical, emotional, mental, and spiritual aspects of their lives to improve their health conditions, we learn the following. Some people get it and take steps to better their health, as they need positive reinforcement and new ideas. Others don't get it but want to, as they struggle to improve but are receptive to help and ideas. Still others don't get it and don't want to, as they are not open to

69

change and want to be left alone. The challenge is to sustain the first group, help the second group, and rather than ignore the third group we need to find ways to help them dissolve their negative core beliefs. Toward this end, we will explore three concepts: awareness, self-actualization, and spiritual transformation.

Awareness, Self-Actualization, and Spiritual Transformation

Our body appears to be composed of solid matter, but quantum physics shows that every atom is 99.9999% empty space, and that subatomic particles are actually bundles of vibrating energy. Mind pervades every cell of our body. Our bodies are really three-dimensional projections of our thoughts. Thoughts and feelings are transformed into molecules, and molecules stimulate thoughts and feelings.

Having an awareness of our need to energize our health, we need personal empowerment not only to improve our health condition but also improve our individual, social, and economic well being as well. Personal empowerment necessitates our exploration of the subconscious and subjective mind. Here we need to examine our core beliefs to see if they are in synchronization with our Islamic beliefs. If not, then we need to reprogram our subconscious mind to bring our core beliefs into harmony with our Islamic beliefs. Otherwise, we become entrapped in our own subconscious core beliefs and have a difficult time in achieving the Islamic personality.

Once personal empowerment is on the right course, then we work towards self-actualization. This is a commitment to move towards a balance and harmony in all aspects of life. We flow in creative and synergistic ways that are compatible with our Islamic spirituality. Toward this end, our self-esteem is heightened; we better understand ourselves, and our perception of the environment and those with whom we come into contact as good. However, self-actualization is not automatic. Unless our lower level needs are fulfilled, we are subconsciously disoriented. Lower level needs must be continuously satisfied to sustain self-actualization.

Satisfying the needs of physical health, emotional health, and mental health will lead us to self-actualization of spiritual health. At times, we have a tendency to relax our spiritual obligations in Islam and fall into the mire of disruptive thinking. When that happens, we need to revisit the lowest level need – physical health – and fulfill all that is required at that level. Once this achieved, then we can satisfy our emotional health and mental health.

Self-actualization is a perpetual process that never ends. It is reinforcement of all our needs to arrive at the realization that our Islamic personality is resolute and secure. Picture an iceberg in the ocean where the tip of the iceberg is resting on the surface of the water and the remainder is under water. The conscious mind is like the tip of the iceberg, while the subconscious mind is like the remainder of the iceberg under water. Our subconscious beliefs are in control of our thoughts and feelings. Spirituality governed by our Islamic personality allows us to dissolve our negative thoughts and feelings.

With personal empowerment and self-actualization, we can now transform our personality into becoming unified within our Islamic spirituality. Our prayers are more focused, as we are immersed in the love and remembrance of God. Transformation means to consciously live unified in body, mind, and soul. At this level of spiritual transformation, we know and live in balance and harmony at all times. In essence, we cleanse our minds of materialistic thoughts and become totally absorbed in our submission to God.

One with the Earth

CHAPTER 5

ENERGY: ENVIRONMENTALISM AND SOVEREIGNTY AS STEWARDSHIP

Islam is considered a comprehensive way of life whose teachings cover every possible human relationship including that with other creatures and the environment. Islam's view of the environment is holistic, in that all elements in nature are connected to each other. Islam provides the means by which to comprehend the natural order and define mankind's responsibility and accountability relative to all creation.

God has given man the faculty of knowledge in order to understand the natural order and purpose of creation. For life to continue, all creation must conform to the natural laws, including but not limited to humanity, plants, animals, water, and all that is included in the cosmos. In our impatience to evolve and progress we have neglected and abused the magnificent nature of Earth and of mankind's place in it.

Concept of Sovereignty

According to Islam, only God is Sovereign and the Absolute Ruler of the whole Universe. The Qur'an describes God as *al-Malik* meaning Sovereign and *al-Malik-ul-Mulk* meaning the Eternal Possessor of Sovereignty. The Qur'an also makes it clear that all power lies in God, Who is *al-Muqtadir* meaning Possessor of All Power:

"For God is He Who gives (all) sustenance, - Lord of Power, - steadfast (forever). (Qur'an 51:58)

The concept of Sovereign is Universal, Transcendental, Indivisible and Absolute. Mankind is allowed limited independence essential to implement and enforce the laws of their Sovereign. As Sovereign, God has conveyed His Divine Law by way of the prophets and holy books, which are the Torah, Psalms, Gospel, and Qur'an. God has appointed man as His vicegerent (*khalifa*) to carry out His Divine Law.

God provides mankind with sustenance and nourishment. (Qur'an 2:21-22) Islam does not make any negative distinction between language and color, as they are perceived as Signs from God:

"And among His Signs is the creation of Heavens and the Earth, and the variations in your languages and your colors: verily in that are Signs for those who know." (Qur'an 30:22)

As there are variations in the colors of people, there are also variations in the colors of animals, plants and inanimate objects (Qur'an 35:27-28). Knowledge allows us to appreciate

73

these variations, while ignorance does not. The same holds true for humanity, which consists of various ethnicities of different colors all belonging to the one human race. People should not harm other people because they are of a different color or race. Similarly, people who have a preference for a particular shape or color of a plant do not abuse or destroy other plants they do not desire. Different shapes and colors are gifts from God to be appreciated and safeguarded. The Unity of Sovereignty derives from the Unity of God (*Tawhid*). The doctrine of Divine Unity implies that none other than God is empowered to exercise sovereign power. When someone claims to possess sovereignty, this contradicts the Divine Unity and the fundamental beliefs of Islam.

Energy is the force that moves the Universe. Energy is everywhere. God's Sovereign Power gave us energy to make our bodies grow and our minds to think. As energy is the ability to do work, animals and inanimate objects can perform simple as well as complex tasks using energy. It is energy that enables us to breathe or to read a book. Similarly, it is energy that enables complex tasks such as launching a rocket into space or the fusion of atoms, but how we utilize this energy determines whether or not we have abused it. God gave us the intellect to protect nature and the environment for the betterment of mankind, plants, animals, and inanimate objects.

Concept of Stewardship

In order to maintain the order of the natural environment, God the Sovereign has appointed humanity as stewards (*khalifa*) on Earth:

"It is He Who hath made you vicegerents of the Earth...." (Qur'an 6:165)

Vicegerency on Earth is based on the principle that humanity's place in creation (*fitra*) is one in which they are the caretakers of the environment in which they dwell. God has given mankind spiritual consciousness so that it can understand nature. As stewards, it is essential for mankind to seek knowledge in order to learn to understand the infinite manifestations of the natural environment. As stewards, humans must be in control at all times and to act with moderation and reason so as not to disrupt the pattern of creation or cause corruption on Earth. As guardians of the Earth, they are perceived as trustees with duties and responsibilities to safeguard and maintain the balance that exists within the environment. As such, they will be held accountable for their actions:

"Then We made you heirs in the land after them, to see how you would behave!" (Qur'an 10:14)

According to Islam, man is but a deputy of God, having no authority except that of a steward. The Islamic underlying principle for an environmental ethic rests steadfastly on the notions of vicegerent and trusteeship (*amana*). God has entrusted man with nature, and the fundamental outcome of man's acceptance of trusteeship is the adjudication of his conduct by Divine Judgment. However, by and large, Muslims have not yet instilled in their consciousness the importance of an ecological ethic or the application of Islamic principles to environmental practice.

While sovereignty belongs to God, it has been delegated in the form of human agency:

"Behold, thy Lord said to the angels: 'I will create a vicegerent on Earth....'" (Qur'an 2:30)

As Sovereign, God determines the codes of conduct and duties and responsibilities man must undertake as God's vicegerent. As God is Sovereign in all affairs, He has exercised His Sovereignty in entrusting some of it to mankind, which must create a society that brings harmony and peace to its inhabitants. Muslims have the freedom to act and as such are accountable for their actions. This accountability follows the person to the Day of Judgment, which is the consequence of human sovereignty.

In an Islamic state, Divine Law determines how the people will administer their governmental affairs. The Sovereignty of God ensures that Divine Law is supreme. While it is mandatory for the head of the Islamic state to serve the people, it is also incumbent upon him to consult with the people in governing the affairs of the state. Both the head of state and the people are required to obey Islamic principles, which forbid tyranny and despotism.

While sovereignty in Islam is to fulfill the Will of God, sovereignty in Western nations is to fulfill the will of its people. While constitutions can be amended, the Qur'an is eternal and open to interpretations based on independent reasoning (*ijtihad*). What distinguishes democracy in Islam from Western democracy is that in Islam democracy rests on the principle of popular vicegerent (*khalifa*) as stewards, while in Western democracy it is based on the concept of popular sovereignty.

In secular democracy, people have the right to make, enact and adjudicate laws. People are sovereign and independent to formulate their own laws based on a democratic constitution. True, in Islamic societies, there are parliaments and legislatures that also make, enact and adjudicate laws, but these laws must be in consonance with the Divine Law.

The Divine Law must be upheld whether for mankind, plants, animals, or inanimate objects, all of which have energy. An inanimate object, stone, lying on the street is an example of energy at rest. It is waiting to be used. It is potential energy. If the stone is picked up and thrown, it moves, and this motion is known as kinetic energy. The main source of energy comes from the sun in the form of radiant energy. Plants convert this radiant energy to chemical energy using the process of photosynthesis. When animals consume food, the chemical energy in food is converted into potential energy in the body. When this energy is used to do work, it becomes kinetic energy. Mankind needs food and water to survive. As stewards, the environment needs to be protected, i.e., plants and animals as well as water and air, so we can nourish our bodies to sustain us. If the environment is abused and neglected, the end result is too catastrophic even beyond our wildest imagination.

Ecological Imperatives

A fundamental necessity of religion is to protect the environment, as espoused by various faiths:

Judaism maintains that God has dominion over the Earth and mankind acts as God's steward to conserve and cultivate the environment (Genesis 2:15) and not to destroy it (Deuteronomy 20:19-20).[53]

Christianity holds the broad ethical view that as neighbors Christians are caretakers, caregivers, and carekeepers of each other (Luke 10:29)[54]

Islam states that God is Sovereign over all creation (Qur'an 2:106), and that mankind is tested as to how well they use what God has provided. In addition, God does not approve of those who spread mischief through the Earth destroying crops and cattle (Qur'an 2:205).

Buddhism stresses great significance towards the protection of the environment on which mankind is dependent upon for survival (Dalai Lama).[55]

Hinduism states that the natural world is sacred with individual spirits (*java*) and a universal consciousness (*Brahman*), and that the Earth should be handled very carefully so as to provide continuous sustenance to its cultivators (Atharva-Veda 12:35).[56]

If these creeds advocate the protection of the environment, then why do we have an ecological crisis? One factor may be that some people have distorted biblical verses in order to satisfy their own schemes and as such have positioned themselves as sovereign over creation. Instead of becoming devoted stewards, they have become destructive forces of not only people but the environment as well, as they incorrectly believe to be sovereign over nature. This desire for power and dominion over the Earth's resources only leads to repression, exploitation and mistreatment of the laws of nature.

The Qur'an makes it clear that as the Earth is our habitat, we must protect it by establishing a balanced way of life without greed or scarcity. This balance (*mizan*) instills justice in creation, because injustice deviates from balance and leads to decay and corruption:

"And the firmament has He raised high, and He has set up the Balance (of Justice), in order that you may not transgress (due) balance. So establish weight with justice and fall not short in the balance." (Qur'an 55:7-9)

Therefore, God created and defined each element in the Universe in due proportion and measure. As balance governs the structure of the Universe, unity is derived from order and harmony. While Islam supports the protection of the environment, it permits opportunity for sustainable development. Destruction to the environment and annihilation of animals are not permitted in Islam. If any species becomes extinct, it upsets the balance of nature. Even hunting for game as fun and sport is deplored in Islam. In Islam, animals are killed only for food and self-defense.

The Qur'an is replete with stories that illustrate the relationship between the behavior of people and the conditions of the environment. Muslims are encouraged to keep the Earth, water and air clean from pollution, as all living things are dependent on them for their existence. Islam even abhors the cutting down of trees, unless for sound and lawful reasons. From various sources, it is stated that Prophet Mohammed had said, *"If you knew that the world would end tomorrow, you should plant a tree."* In short, the destruction of the environment prevents mankind from fulfilling the concept of vicegerency on Earth.

Protecting the environment also draws us to protect inanimate objects, such as stones and rocks. Even the basest of objects, a stone lacking feeling, sensation, and reproduction, is still endowed with the trait of unusual durability and hardness. Everything which we see, and even that which we do not see, holds energy. Inanimate, or solid objects, have a denser concentration of energy which is what makes them solid. We are used to imagining energy as being fluid, and so may find it more difficult to think of inanimate objects in this way.

In Islam, there is a mutual relationship between man's self-improvement and the improvement of his environment. In this regard man, as steward, must constantly strive to improve his way of life that is in balance with his endeavor to protect and enhance the environment he lives in. The protection of the natural environment is an imperative ordered by God. As man strives for perfection in his life, he also prepares himself for reconstructing his environment.

Islam stresses the importance of righteousness and does not allow for deviant behavior and corruption that result in the destruction of the social system and the safety of its people and the environment. God said, *"And O my people! Give just measure and weight, nor withhold from the people the things that are their due: commit not evil in the land with intent to do mischief."* (Qur'an 11:85) Toward this end, man must make a concerted effort to not only build his character in consonance with the establishment and preservation of a just social system but also to put an end to those who wish to destroy that system.

Solutions

To formulate effective solutions for the environmental crisis, we must place them within the broader historical, societal and cultural setting. This requires a mass transformation and radical change in our values as to how we live. In Islam, practical solutions to the environmental dilemma lie in man's leadership and guidance relative to the principles, laws and institutions of the society. Some suggestions follow:

- Preservation of the natural environment is an ethical imperative that necessitates continuous education, scientific research, technical competence and effective legislation.

- Religious leaders from various faiths, in conjunction with other institutions and the United Nations Environment Programme (UNEP), need to work jointly so as to define, intensify, and adapt value systems and moral ethics to the shifting and pervasive hazards of the environment within the framework of public policy, global relations, economic systems and individual behavior.[57]

- Narrow the gap between religious customs and science by increasing the capacity for moral reflection and cultural diversity on environmental issues so that religious leaders can act on the knowledge that science provides them.

- Nations must work in consonance with each other so as to protect the natural environment from exploitation, irreparable damage or hostile behavior.

- .Promote a fundamental, shared ecological ethic that would reassess the purpose of the natural environment in our global society and our methods for evaluating it.

Islam supports all ecological endeavors on a global scale for preserving and restoring our natural environment. In this respect, we are faced with the endless challenge to mobilize our resources for the purpose of sustaining and enjoying good health and prosperity. Here Islam instills a sense of sacredness within the natural world, as it provides the required religious knowledge and understanding that advocates a transformation to environmental ethics. As some of the causes of our dilemma are religious, then part of the solution must be fundamentally religious.

A case example of what Islam is doing to safeguard the natural environment can be demonstrated by the Islamic Foundation for Ecology and Environmental Sciences, located in England. The Foundation has established an extensive training program in environmental teachings based on the Qur'an. For example, the Foundation promotes self-sufficiency in farming through organic agriculture and perm culture. The Foundation also establishes centers of community living that show Islam as an integrated pattern of productive social life working in harmony with nature. Some of the Foundation's projects include (a) revitalization of the

Indonesian environmental movement through the application of Islamic environmental ethics; (b) sensitizing Muslims in Nigeria to the ethical dimensions of Islamic environmental practice; (c) re-greening areas in Pakistan based on Islamic conservation principles; (d) laying down foundations of Islamic environmental practice in Tanzania; and (e) rehabilitation of traditional water conservation systems in Yemen through the application of Islamic conservation principles.[58]

In order to have ecological coexistence, religions and cultures must make a proactive contribution towards safeguarding the Earth and its resources. Additionally, in order to lessen the ecological crisis, science and technology can help find ways to improve upon the environment so that the poor have a chance to survive. As enormous advances have taken place in science and technology to the benefit of mankind, these developments have also created enormous problems and health hazards, threatening the survival of human life. While science and technology are needed to advance the preservation of the natural environment, they must be controlled so as not to overcome man's spiritual consciousness that can lead to the destruction of the natural balance.

We must also find ways to address other factors that impinge on the environment, such as consumerism, shifting cultivation, land rotation and industrialization. In order to develop a healthy and sustainable Earth, the public needs to be continuously educated relative to the preservation of the environment, be it farming or agro-forestry. As Islam encourages moderation relative to human nature and life, it discourages an extravagant lifestyle that leads to weakness among individuals and nations.

Eco-development brings about social and economic justice while at the same time improving upon living conditions.[59] Consequently, man must be accountable, for it is accountability that links ethics and rationality. Without accountability, ethics is weak. Ethics must flow from our profound insight into the linkage between life and the prudence we attribute to the environment. How this comes about is when religions and cultures cooperate and live in peace and harmony. That is why interfaith dialogue is so important. It affords us a tool to better understand each other and to establish a common ecological ethic towards working together for equity and sustenance. Mostly in this way we can truly become the stewards that the Sovereign God intended us to be.

The world is constantly changing, and Islam can join with other faiths to create a vision of an environmental society. Sovereignty declares that only God has ownership of the Earth. Mankind's purpose is one of stewardship entrusted by God to ensure that the Earth is nurtured and cultivated for the purpose of sustaining mankind. This trusteeship takes on the added responsibility of protecting the environment from waste, pollution or destruction of its natural resources.

As God has made mankind His stewards, they need to become more culturally, technologically, and environmentally innovative and dynamic. Muslims must recognize their ethical and practical accountability relative to the preservation of the Earth and the elimination of poverty. If Muslims are to develop sustainable environmental communities, they must also eradicate oppression and terrorism that give rise to destruction of both people and the natural resources. Muslims can overcome these frailties by instilling in their persona the virtue of tolerance that Islam mandates for each Muslim.

The Laws of Islam (*Shariah*) provide a foundation in which man can fulfill the role of trustee. These Laws establish ethical guidelines to counteract the disruption in human life brought about by the severe ecological crises. While the Laws of Islam do in fact pertain to nature, their practice has been somewhat limited or ignored. Qur'anic verses underscore the importance of environmental ethics and mankind's obligation as stewards to protect the environment. Toward this end, Muslims must pay heed to the Qur'an by also studying it from an ecological perspective.

Rather than being God's steward to protect nature, man has violated that trust by taking the position of dominator repeatedly ignoring revelation. Man must utilize the intelligence that God has given him so that he can interact with nature in a way that is worthy of this intelligence. As steward, he must fulfill the responsibility that the Sovereign God has given him. Therefore, mankind must join forces to make this world a better and safer place to live in. Otherwise, the dreadful remedy to the environmental dilemma may be global war!

KA'BAH IN MECCA

CHAPTER 6

ENERGIZING THE ISLAMIC PERSONALITY

The Qur'an generates waves of vibrant energy, and each wave brings forth the enlightenment of knowledge and guidance. The more knowledge we gain in Islam the greater the intensity of these vibrant waves. High frequency waves generate high intensity. Therefore, the greater the frequency of these waves the greater the intensity. Energy fields permeate through the Qur'an and the rate of vibrant energy within each field is directly proportional to the speed in which one becomes more enlightened.

Muslims understand the verses in the Qur'an according to their intellect, which means that some verses may have deeper meaning for the more pious and knowledgeable Muslims than for those who are not as pious and knowledgeable. Therefore, vibrant energy has a more profound radiation on the more pious and knowledgeable Muslims. As Muslims become immersed in the faith of Islam, their grip on the Rope of God strengthens.

According to Jameel Kermalli in his book, entitled *Islam the Absolute Truth: A Comprehensive Approach to Understanding Islam's Beliefs and Practices*, it is clear that if one's energy field is pure, the conscious part of it is unadulterated, and with higher vibratory frequencies he or she is in a much better position to understand and reflect on the verses of the Qur'an.[60] It is assumed that interaction with the energy from the Divine verses increases communication with God. That is why it is important to have deep concentration when reciting the verses from the Qur'an, in order to sustain the Muslim's higher rate of vibration.

Significance of the *Rope of God*

We achieve self-actualization when we reinforce and strengthen our grip to the *Rope of God*, as we adhere to the fundamental virtues of Islam: Articles of Faith and Branches of Faith. There are three major categories of the Articles of Faith (belief in the Oneness of God, the Prophets, and the Hereafter). The belief in the Unity of God, the Justice of God, the Angels, the Imamat (succession to Prophet Mohammad), and the Books of God derive from these three major categories. For example, the Books of God are revealed to the Prophets who in turn deliver God's Divine Revelation to mankind. The Branches of Faith are many. Some of them are prayer, fasting, alms, pilgrimage and struggle (*jihad*). Yet, other virtues interweave with these founding principles, such as tolerance, generosity, righteous deeds, truth and patience. Reinforcement and strengthening of these virtues are accomplished by way of cleanliness both of the external self as well as of the internal self. The concept of *weaved ropes* is intertwined within the *Rope*, as our grip is strengthened by each strand. This grip is reinforced by our Islamic personality, which resonates within our spirituality.

83

And what do we reference and follow in order to understand the nature of these virtues as well as how to conduct ourselves accordingly? To begin with, we have the Qur'an, which is the *Rope of God*, and it is extended to include *Ahl al-Bayt* (Household of Prophet Mohammad) and the *Sunnah* (traditions and lifestyle of Prophet Mohammad). This transcends into the proper attitude and behavior for Muslims to follow. The end result of the *Rope* is the truth of certainty for unity must prevail.

The *Rope* energizes and becomes fully executable, for example, when Muslims at the Hajj (pilgrimage) meet and pray in unity, or when they bind together in their struggle to enjoin good and prohibit evil, or when they congregate at a funeral to bury the deceased. The *Rope* is the vehicle that determines if one is to go to Heaven or to Hell. The stronger the *Rope* the easier it is to drive on to Heaven. The weaker the *Rope* the more difficult it is to find Heaven's road. The symbolism is that of a *Rope* hanging down from Heaven to Earth so that by holding it, believers may climb up to Heaven.

There is even a kind of rope that starts with conception. Babies receive nourishment and oxygen in the womb through the placenta, which is connected to the inner wall of the mother's uterus. The placenta is connected to the baby by the umbilical cord through an opening in the baby's stomach. After the baby is born, the umbilical cord is clamped and cut close to the body in a painless procedure, leaving an umbilical stump. Within a few weeks, the stump will dry up and drop off; leaving a small wound that may take a few days to heal. The meaning of the *Rope* here is that it begins from conception to birth to life's journey of trials and tribulations. For each of us is tested on how well we cling to that *Rope* and prepare ourselves for the Hereafter. A major test is that of prayer, as nourishment for the soul like the umbilical cord is nourishment for the fetus.

Rope of God Energizes Muslims

Here are some examples of how the *Rope of God* energizes Muslims:

- People aligned in unity at the congregational Friday Prayer or Holiday Prayer asking for God's Blessing. The energy that emits from each Muslim resonates into one unified force, as each clings to a strand of the personified *Rope*.

- Fasting during the month of Ramadan requires deep concentration in order to complete each day of the fast. Great concentration is needed as we pray the obligatory five prayers each day to remind us of our commitment to Islam. Refraining from idle gossip, backbiting, profane language, and pessimism helps strengthen the *Rope* and complete our fulfillment to Islam.

- In the string of charitable undertakings, Muslims should not boast about their good deeds. Rather, concentration should be on seeking additional ways to partake in charitable causes. Toward this end, positive energy overcomes the negative energy of boasting.

- Kinetic energy (movement) is best personified during the Hajj (pilgrimage). The movement of Muslims in their circumambulation at the Ka'bah is like a *Rope* that encircles the shrine. If the energy of their faith is strong, they will have no problem in holding fast to the *Rope,* as they encircle around the Ka'bah unified as one. If their faith is weak, the *Rope* will feel slippery and their hands will slide away. Like an electromagnetic energy center, the Ka'bah resonates within and strengthens the inner being of every Muslim, as they perform their circumambulation. During the circumambulation, as the Muslims make their intention to cleanse themselves of their sins, the Black Stone at the Ka'bah draws the negative energy from them to purify their souls. Many Muslims believe that the Black Stone was once a pure and dazzling white stone, but that it became black because of the sins it has absorbed from the Muslims over the centuries. However, there are Muslims who believe that the Black Stone can only erase the believer's minor sins.

- Our struggle (*jihad*) is also part of the *Rope*. As we struggle to do good and prohibit evil, and as we struggle to suppress our ego, we are doing so in order to hold fast to the *Rope*. Division within ourselves occurs when we compromise our Islamic morals and values or when materialism is our priority. Unity with each other occurs when we are steadfast and put our reliance on God for His Gratitude, Generosity, Gentleness and Patience.

In short, we are in spiritual harmony with each other when we have unity within ourselves, within our family, and within our community. Unity is the basis of Islam. The Unity of God, the unity of brotherhood, the unity of purpose, and the unity of action are often mentioned in the Qur'an. Unity makes it possible to create strong ties with each other in order to achieve God's Blessing. To achieve this unity, it is patience and wisdom that make us realize that we have many more things in common than we have differences. Prophet Mohammad had said:

"God likes three things for you and hates three things for you. He likes for you that you should worship Him; that you should not associate any partner with Him; and that you should hold fast to the Rope of God all together and not be divided among yourselves. He dislikes for you to have much talk and arguments; the plentiful questioning and asking; and the waste and destruction of wealth or property."

Holding fast (*I'atisaam*) to the *Rope of God* protects us from misguidance and destruction. Holding fast also protects us from deviation. Holding fast is to attain the Shelter and Protection of God. Holding fast is to self-actualize in spirituality and to deny any attachment to materialism. To achieve the Islamic personality and morality with the best of manners and conduct is purification of the soul that strengthens the grip of the *Rope*. And what better way to achieve this than to prostrate in prayer in order to be nearer to our Lord. A major artery of the *Rope* is prayer. There is no substitute for prayer. No matter how many good deeds are done in one's lifetime, the combined weight of all these good deeds will not equal the weight of one prayer. How each person fares with respect to good and evil will determine their strength within the *Rope*.

Fasting during the month of Ramadan affords us the golden opportunity of focused reflection and action. We need to reflect on how to unite the *Ummah* (Muslim community). We need to be nurtured with the ideals of discipline and sincerity as we move towards activating the unity. Without unity we lose sight of Islam and the community becomes lost. With the individual, there is unity of interaction with virtues. With the family, there is unity of trust and tolerance. With peer groups, there is unity of gentleness and understanding. With the community, there is unity of working together to build a better society. With the nation, there is unity in diversity. With the world, there is unity of security and peace. With the Universe, there is unity of the Cosmos.

For true unity, let us all hold fast to the *Rope of God*. During the month of Ramadan, we must become more focused and our senses heightened towards virtues such as piety, humility, forgiveness, generosity and forbearance. We must practice self-restraint on that which is against Islam. Fasting becomes our struggle and resistance against evil, and with prayer we are guided to the straight path of purity. Unity maximizes on energy, and we need to demonstrate our commitment to Islam by fulfilling our Islamic obligations.

In order to cling to the *Rope of God*, we should set free our narrow perceptions and biases and overcome obstinacy. We need to contain our ego in order to set free our suspicions, doubts and fallacies. We need not have predetermined notions of what should be or what should not be but, rather, to let our hearts and innermost self speak out. The self-will and obstinacy put us in a state of confusion, as they overpower the heart and lead us into temptation and misery. We need to hold steadfast to truth and love in order to achieve self-fulfillment.

If we are to cling tenaciously to the *Rope*, then we must find the way to energize ourselves and hold fast to each strand and to each knot. This energy must allow the heavenly flow of creativity and wisdom into our hearts and minds. Holding fast to the *Rope* unleashes our innermost fears, anxieties and weaknesses. People oftentimes demand respect from others rather than earning it. They insist on being respected even to the point of overpowering others to get it. Respect cannot flourish in a clogged-up system that detonates from mistrust, power and falsification of truth. With an open energy system we can positively create fulfillment and enrichment within ourselves.

Family Unity and Self

Strong families recognize that there are benefits and pleasures to be gained from time and activities together. By spending time together, families build a reserve of good feelings and are able to cope with personal and family crisis more effectively. Strong families are deeply committed to the family unit and to promoting the happiness and welfare of each other. Family commitment comes from an active involvement in setting and carrying out family goals. Family unity encourages families to create daily routines as well as special traditions and celebrations that affirm members, connect them to their family roots, and add fun to ordinary family events. Family unity includes time that family members spend together. Family unity means maintaining family identity and togetherness and balancing family priorities with support for individual needs. Family unity produces strong family bonds and freedom for individual self-expression.

Families are products of the community that weaves them, and they transmit the social strengths and weaknesses of those larger social institutions. Family experiences shapes development of individual and collective consciousness. Persons and family systems carry within them the roots of identity that involves genetics, culture, spirit and emotion. At least these four core elements are keys to self-knowledge. The resulting construct of identity, for both families and individuals, is the lens through which human existence and experience is filtered and defined. Beginning to learn about one's heritage can help facilitate self-awareness as a member of a family. This provides the bridge to a cultural base, empowering individuals and family systems to confirm or reweave their values, identify patterns, and make changes in personal, family and cultural activities.

Enlightenment

In Islam, we are to question and use our faculties of reason in order to find absolute truth. There is no blind following or imitation. One must always question his values to make sure they are in accordance with the Divine Law as stated in the Qur'an. It is impossible for reason to extend beyond the boundaries of Islam, because there is no contradiction between reason and Islam. On the contrary, reason of the mind leads one to the path of Islam.

As Muslims, we are encouraged to overcome ignorance by seeking knowledge from the cradle to the grave. Before Islam, man was to limit himself and his mind. When faced with a contradiction in dogma, he was told to follow the law strictly by faith and negate reason. This imprisoned man's soul. Islam opened the gate to reason, stating that all knowledge and truth emanate from God; therefore, an unbiased search for truth and knowledge leads one directly to the path of Islam. Islam does not place a boundary. Islam is the epitome of reason. It is God Who is the Giver of Enlightenment.

To be enlightened in Islam means to gain spiritual insight and knowledge in the search for truth, understanding and wisdom. This search takes on a commitment in one's mind, and it can only come about through one's endurance and patience. Enlightenment is not ignorance. Enlightenment is based on free will and independent intellect. Ignorance, on the other hand, is darkness. The religion of Islam gave us a new perspective of enlightenment. This allowed man to better understand himself while at the same time liberating him from ignorance and confusion. Therefore, man was now able to restore his self-dignity and self-identity.

Self-Concept

The self-concept has a powerful influence on one's behavior, perhaps, the most powerful influence. Man has a basic tendency to strive, actualize, maintain and enhance himself:

"Man gets only what he strives for." (Qur'an 53:39)

The person develops this self-concept in order to gain confidence and feel good about him. There are boundaries that one must not extend beyond. The danger of enhancing one's self-concept outside the parameters of Islam, for example, an egotist, miser, gambler, drunkard, to mention just a few, renders that person a failure in his faith. Therefore, man's self-concept is one that strives toward the goal of patience and perfection in Islam, and one of the ways this is achieved is by performing good deeds:

"As for those who strive for Our Cause, We will definitely guide them to Our Paths...." (Qur'an 29:69)

As we strive hard to have a deeper understanding of our purpose in life, we need to reflect on what is good. Toward this end, we seek guidance from God to help us. We must work hard to prioritize our goals and to make a sincere and honest effort to leave what is forbidden and adopt what is good. To be focused in understanding our inner self helps to better understand the principles of Islam, which will improve our self-concept and find ourselves peaceful and contented. Reaching the straight path must have clarity of mind that is sincere and ready to change oneself toward the good. As we strive to be righteous, God will guide us toward this end.

Self-Esteem

Controlling self-esteem shapes and molds one's self-concept. Developing positive self-esteem means to regard life and its surroundings with respect and affection. We become more positive about our feelings for ourselves. As our opinion of ourselves improves, we become better Muslims as well. People with high self-esteem take risks, and each risk they take teaches them something. Risk, however, requires patience.

Self-esteem is an extremely powerful factor in our growth and development as Muslims. To grow in Islam, we must practice endurance. Part of that endurance and power comes from its uniqueness. It operates as a mechanism for maintaining our inner consistency. It helps determine how our experiences are interpreted. It provides a set of expectancies - what we do in situations and how we interpret what others do in situations.

Self-Fulfillment

Becoming the best we can, as Muslims require a commitment and the patience to succeed. We need to be committed towards working up to our potential to learn and understand the concepts of Islam. This results in self-fulfillment and self-satisfaction. Knowledge and understanding give direction for one to realize his objectives and goals, while wisdom enhances one's self-fulfillment to its fullest potential:

"...For God has sent down to you the Book and Wisdom and taught you what you knew not...." (Qur'an 4:113)

And truth is the light that enlightens one's mind and keeps him or her on the straight path. When self-fulfillment comes into balance with the self-concept the end result is self-esteem, the ultimate in happiness. Just as man needs to come into balance with his society, so does self-fulfillment need to come into balance with the self-concept. The way to achieve this balance is by way of self-esteem, the basis of which is intellectual enlightenment and the zenith of which is patience. This balance gives the person an integrated self, a higher standard of perfection. What emanates from this integration is the value of truth. And this truth allows one to fulfill his submission to God. Men and women who accept the guidance of truth will purify their minds and bodies:

"...Now Truth has come to you from Your Lord! Those who receive Guidance do so for the good of their own souls; those who stray do so to their own loss...." (Qur'an 10:108)

Criteria for Developing Islamic Self

When we come to learn and understand the balance and equilibrium of energy within our body's system, we gain an entirely new perspective about ourselves. We begin to understand the meaning of unity within the self. So how can we create, nurture, and then effectively use this perspective to help us be better Muslims?

- *Be patient*:   Self-discovery, self-development, self-awareness, self-esteem, and self-confidence take time to acquire. One thing we can do is to try giving away of ourselves. Instead of pulling everything towards ourselves, allow things to go out from us. When we make important connections with others through our commitments, attention, time, respect, and attitudes toward them, we will be defining ourselves by what we are giving to them. Patience will help us be what we want to be, because attainment is within reach if we persevere. But, remember, patience is not passive; on the contrary it is active; it is concentrated strength.

- *Be purposeful*: Have a goal; have a set of goals. Plan and have alternative plans as well. What we do while in the process of becoming not only can influence what we become, but it can provide a clearer definition of what we want to be. So plan our work and work our plan, because the one who fails to plan is planning to fail!

- *Be persistent*:   Stick with our perspective.   In today's society, we want instant gratification. Why? Because everything appears to be instant - instant coffee, instant potatoes, instant winners, and instant rewards. Self-fulfillment through one's perspective is not instant. Becoming who we want to be is not instant. The only thing about it that is instant is when we can start. We cannot do everything at once; but we can do something at once!

Controlling the Islamic self is not an easy task. It requires control of one's inner thoughts and actions. Becoming enlightened in Islam is to understand one's self-concept, control one's self-esteem, and attain self-fulfillment by way of patience, purposefulness, and persistence. Control is achieved by way of order and harmony within the self. The Cosmos is the systematic order, harmony, and unity within the Universe, as well as within a society, institution, and family and above all within oneself.

Ego - Threat to Self

Whether one is egoistic or egotistic, he is morally depraved and suffers from false impressions of himself. This self-centeredness and self-absorption within himself immensely diminishes his chances of ever reaching moral fulfillment and self-respect. Keeping occupied with thoughts and actions of materialism, greed, center of attention and conceit, he continues to fall deeper and deeper into a spiral pit of which he cannot escape. This obedience to his self further erodes his soul, as he commits every act of transgression, deception and sedition in order to achieve his superiority or authority over others. In a nutshell, he begins to worship himself thereby becoming totally impervious to spirituality and the common good.

The person who is continually boasting about himself is someone whose self-worth is meaningless, and he feels the necessity to tap other avenues or sources to restore his self-esteem. This need for replenishment is vital since the ego functions out of fear. The ego operates in such a way so as to give the egotist a sense of loneliness and separation from the world. The egotist feels he is obliged to act the way he does since no one really cares about him. This leads him constantly seeking approval in any way he can get it. His addiction to his inner self makes him even more anxious to not only seek approval from others but to demand it as well. The end result is that the egotist finds himself rejected by others. Still the egotist revitalizes himself and seeks other means for acceptance, even if it means engaging in corruption and immoral acts to achieve it.

How a Muslim fulfills his needs is by devoting himself to spirituality and not to vanity and conceit. Spirituality helps mold one's personality and sets the individual on the right track. Vanity and conceit severely limit the person's strive for self-worth, thereby resulting in humiliation and disgrace. With humility and self-sacrifice, one can recover his sense of worth and regain his spirituality free of pride and complacency. There is no room for selfish ambition or vain conceit or self-delusions. Those who have a superior attitude that they are always right portray this kind of approach. They confront others to prove their point, and they must have the final say in all matters. Rather than recognizing their mistake, they keep on pressing forward against those who support truth. For the egotists, they feel that those who oppose them are rivals. But the real rival is the rival within them.

With a lack of unity within one's self, the egotist becomes weak, suffers from low morale, and consumes his energy focusing on trivial issues and problems. This in turn leads to personality clashes and enmity. The egotist is ignorant about his obligation to strive for unity within himself and within others. The love of this life and the propensity to control others are reasons for discord. To combat egotism, we must have a strong sense of solidarity and brotherhood whereby we better understand one another and work towards the common good. We must cling to the *Rope of God* with every ounce of energy and determination to succeed.

Self-Forgiveness

Forgiveness is an attribute that has received much discussion in Islam. The self-realization of forgiveness is when one is willing to forgive when he has the power to take revenge. Forgiveness is an acknowledgment of a person's pledge to not inflict any more harm on anyone, and to make a concerted effort to remedy his inner self towards one of peace and harmony. Toward this end, forgiveness benefits both the one who harms as well as the one who is harmed.

"And hasten unto (the means to obtain) forgiveness from your Lord and Paradise vast as the Heavens and the Earth, prepared for the pious ones. Those who spend (in alms) alike in prosperity and straightness, and who restrain (their) anger, and forgive (the faults of) men; for God loveth those who do good (to others)." (Qur'an 3:133-134)

One of the Attributes of God is that He is Forgiving. As God Forgives, it is necessary for humans to forgive as well. When we pardon others for their inequities and harm against us, we reach the highest level of forgiveness. We cleanse and emancipate ourselves from the evils of Satan. Forgiving one's enemies is a hallmark of self-respect.

Self-Criticism

Self-criticism (*muhasaba*) is a necessary requirement for one to bring his thoughts and actions in harmony with righteousness. A righteous Muslim constantly evaluates his actions and seeks improvement in order to bring him closer to God. The Muslim becomes unified within his self by overcoming his inner weaknesses of sins and deviant behavior. Through self-criticism, one can seek and discover his spirituality. By reaching the spiritual level, one can make amends for past mistakes and seek forgiveness from God. Self-criticism is one of the most difficult deeds to perform. It takes an enormous effort to evaluate and take account for one's own deeds. Repentance follows the awareness of one's mistakes. This awareness is a direct result of constant self-criticism, which is a prerequisite for achieving piety:

"O you who believe! Fear God, and let every soul look to what (provision) he has sent forth for the morrow. Yes, fear God: for God is well acquainted with (all) that you do." (Qur'an 59:18)

This verse commands us to practice self-restraint and avoid committing sins. We should always strive to please God by evaluating our inner selves so that we can be righteous. Self-criticism brings us closer to God, as it intensifies and heightens our piety. Self-criticism acts like an alarm system. It can alert a person as to whether something is good or evil. Hopefully, the person engages in self-criticism in order to avert committing an evil action. Through self-criticism, one is able to attain peace and tranquility.

Before one criticizes someone else, he should first criticize himself. Perpetual self-criticism allows one to move closer to perfection in his faith. Self-criticism may precede an action or it may follow an action. For example, one may evaluate his inner self before making his intention so as to commit a good act. If it is not a good act, then he rejects it. Even if the act is a good one, the believer will always consider if that act will please God. Always the believer holds the self to be accountable for all actions. This, of course, requires the believer to be sincere, obedient to God, and to follow the example of Prophet Mohammad. Islam encourages self-criticism in order for us to call ourselves to account before God does. As self-criticism is the first step in repentance, we need to constantly evaluate and re-evaluate how we have spent our time each day.

Self and the Islamic Personality

Within our personality structure, we have individual selves. Each of these selves has a unique system. For example, the self has its own goals and priorities. Each has its own perceptions and motives. Each has its own style and developmental cycles. Each has its own limits of tolerance and emotional sensitivity. Dynamic and interactive, our sub-selves can communicate with each other to form a decision. When making decisions, the sub-selves condition our true basic self.

We are not born with a personality. Our personality is formed, shaped and developed in the framework of our relationships with our family and environment. Personality is consistency of individuality, as we behave in a manner consistent within each of us. It is this consistency of our behavior that defines the kind of personality we are associated with.

People often see themselves differently from how others perceive them. How one sees oneself is what is referred to as the self-concept, which can be either positive or negative. A positive self-concept results in one feeling good, while a negative self-concept results in one feeling bad. The self-concept consists of one's thoughts, attitudes and feelings about himself, i.e., his perceived self worth. What have a bearing on one's self-concept are such factors as education, religion, family background, and overall health.

The basic self-concept is the person's concept of what he is. The person arrives at this after considering such things as his physical appearance, strengths or weaknesses, position in a community, values, and aspirations. The ideal self-concept, however, consists of ideas of what one would like to be or what he believes he ought to be. It may be realistic in the sense that it is within reach or unrealistic if it is out of reach. For example, he may want to be a physician but has not prepared academically for that career. Or he may want to be a professional football player but does not have the size, strength, speed, and agility to become one.

Family influences the development of the personality both directly and indirectly. The parents use reinforcements such as rewards and punishments to make their teachings effective. One indirect influence is role modeling. Here the child identifies with and emulates the behavior of an older family member. As a result, the child is likely to develop desirable or undesirable personality traits as he or she tries to mimic the behaviors of the admired family member. Another direct influence is the deliberate effort parents make in molding the child's behaviors to conform to societal expectations. Even technology, for example, the emerging information society, has an impact on the human mind and personality. Increasing the use of technology could have a negative influence on the human mind. However, the appropriate use of technology could have a significant benefit for the whole society.

Development of the Islamic Personality

We need to develop unity within ourselves by holding fast onto the *Rope of God*. One of the ways in which we can achieve this is by developing an Islamic personality:

"Therefore, be patient with what they say and celebrate (constantly) the praises of the Lord, before the rising of the sun, and before its setting; yea, celebrate them for part of the hours of the night and at the sides of the day: that thou may have (spiritual) joy." (Qur'an 20:130)

Evil hovers around us. We must be patient and ask God for Guidance so that we can avoid evil. The Islamic personality makes the believer cherish his human dignity and prestige and accept his responsibilities as a Muslim. The best example of the Islamic personality is that of Prophet Mohammad and his progeny.

The justification of religious morality, that is, Islamic morality promises the continuance of life in the Hereafter for the morally good individuals. In Islam, there is no distinction between theoretical morality and physical morality. Morality deals with determining right from wrong. Morality is comprised of virtues. Faith, righteous deeds, truth and patience are the basic virtues of Islamic morality. Man gains eternal happiness through moral virtues.

Islam is a faith that is based on cleanliness:

"...God loveth those who turn unto Him constantly and loveth those who clean themselves." (Qur'an 2:222)

Cleanliness here does not just refer to our daily washing and cleansing of our bodies. There is a higher meaning to this message, a meaning that attaches itself to the inner purity of the soul. We must cleanse our thoughts and our hearts in order to attain ultimate and final perfection. In striving towards perfection through self-purification, God will guide us:

"And those who strive in Our (Cause) - We will certainly guide them to Our Paths: for verily God is with those who do good." (Qur'an 29:69)

And the path is the straight path (*sirat al-mustakim*). We must free ourselves from the spider's web of this frail world. We must walk the path of struggle against immoral tendencies. All that we can do is to strive in the way of God. With firmness of purpose, determination and patience we can attain the Mercy of God.

In addition to cleanliness, there are other traits that help nurture one's Islamic personality. For example, while the ideal Islamic personality is one of moral excellence, it is also the preservation of self-respect and dignity by way of piety. It is one of righteousness and faith. It is one of adhering to the beliefs and practices in Islam. For example one studies the rules of Hajj

94

before making the pilgrimage. When he returns from the Hajj, his awareness is heightened, his soul is purified, and his lifestyle exemplifies that of a Muslim.

The ideal Islamic personality is one who believes his sole purpose in life is to worship God, and to seek the Pleasure and Guidance of God. The ideal Islamic personality is one where faith leads to good deeds and good deeds lead to faith. By helping others he is in effect helping himself become a better Muslim. He sincerely concentrates on every aspect of his life, as he continues to understand the beauty and wisdom of Islam. He reads the Qur'an so that he can be enlightened, and he is grateful for the bounties and blessings God has bestowed upon him. Therefore, he continues to remember God and to win the satisfaction of the Creator.

Revolving Hierarchy of the Islamic Personality

As a guideline, I formulated the Revolving Hierarchy of the Islamic Personality, which begins with faith (*iman*) and ends with patience (*sabr*) and then proceeds back to faith (*iman*) by way of cleanliness. This is based on the four virtues in the Qur'anic chapter entitled 'Asr, which inculcates within mankind the four primary virtues of faith, righteous deeds, truth, and patience. Imam Ali said:

"...*Practice endurance and patience; it is to faith what the head is to the body. There is no good in a body without a head, or in faith without endurance.*" (Nahjul Balagah: Saying #82)[61]

Tantamount to this circular effect is the analogy of proceeding from theory to fact and then back to theory again. The following diagram illustrates the revolving impact of energy on the various stages of the self leading to perfecting the Islamic personality:

Revolving Hierarchy of the Islamic Personality

The six groups are: (1) self-foundation (*asas an-nafs*); (2) self-security (*aman an-nafs*); (3) self-awareness (*waee an-nafs*); (4) self-achievement (*tahkeek an-nafs*); (5) self-satisfaction (*retha an-nafs*); and (6) self-realization (*idrak an-nafs*). In the Arabic language, faith is known as *iman* and patience is known as *sabr*. The Revolving Hierarchy is circular in that it begins with faith (self-foundation) and ends with patience (self-realization) and then proceeds back from patience to faith.

There are at least two theories as to how we absorb these criteria. One theory given by a number of religious scholars is that God makes these and other criteria prior to our existence. And that in our lives we practice the criteria that God has already given us at birth. Another theory postulated by several scholars is that we are not given these criteria at birth but, rather, we develop these criteria as we progress in our lives. What this means is that we choose during our lives whether to develop some or all of these criteria. Each theory complements the other, as God has given us the human mind to think and act. The measurement of how we utilize the capacity of our mind is how well we follow the guidance from God relative to our obligations, such as truth and justice. What is important in either theory is that we can practice these criteria according to the values and virtues given us by God. As we search for meaning in our lives, it is these values and virtues that make for a better Islamic personality.

These criteria of the Islamic personality are intertwined with each other. Self-foundation is the basic need, while self-security and self-awareness are deficit needs. Self-achievement, self-satisfaction and self-realization are growth needs. As these needs are dependent on each other, they cannot be separated. They comprise the total Islamic personality. For example, assume that we have progressed to the growth need of self-satisfaction and suddenly the deficit need of self-security is threatened. Therefore, we have to regress back in the hierarchy and fulfill the deficit need of self-security. Growth needs must be pursued once the requirements of the lower needs are fulfilled.

With faith as the self-foundation, we proceed upward until we attain self-realization by way of patience, and then we proceed back to faith. We always need to reinforce and strengthen our Islamic personality by absorbing ourselves in these criteria.

Having faith leads us to practice and be secure in at least the five requirements of prayer, fasting, alms, pilgrimage and struggle. With this we become aware of knowledge as we seek truth, understanding and wisdom. Piety results in the self-achievement of the straight path, righteous deeds, worship, and prosperity. Happiness emanates from self-satisfaction and occurs when man has freed himself from selfishness and basic desires. One who is purified through piety and is humble and patient will attain prosperity, happiness and tranquility:

"O you who believe! Persevere in patience and constancy; vie in such perseverance; strengthen each other; and fear God; that you may prosper." (Qur'an 3:200)

At the zenith of the fulfillment of these needs is self-realization through patience. Similarly, moving from patience downward through each of the six categories makes us more cognizant of our role as Muslims and of our contribution towards Islam.

Moral judgment is applied to all activities of man, which results in a single undivided Islamic personality. Through prayer, we can strengthen our Islamic personality and resolve in order to grapple with evil and overcome its dastardly venom. Struggle (*jihad*) manifests itself in prayer. True, God provides sustenance for all, just and unjust, in this ephemeral world. But this is a transient existence that ends almost as soon as it begins. So be prudent and wise in how we utilize that sustenance, and exercise our patience and struggle in the way of God by doing good and prohibiting evil.

The Muslim has to protect his external behavior and his deeds, his words and his thoughts, his feelings and his intentions. Truth is his goal. According to al-Ghazali, the highest function of the soul is to perceive the truth.[62] Justice will prevail. Every soul must return to God for His Justice and Judgment. Life in this world is very short; however, life in the Hereafter is eternal. God provides sustenance to the righteous in the Hereafter. In the physical world, we can lead a life of happiness; however, real happiness is in the Hereafter. There is a strong relationship between faith and the nature of this world, as our deeds will affect us either positively or negatively. Performing good deeds in our physical life will prepare us well for happiness in the Hereafter, whereas bad deeds will lead to a dark and ghastly Hereafter of punishment.

The Holy Quran

CHAPTER 7

SELECTED EXAMPLES OF ENERGY
IN THE QUR'AN

The Qur'an is replete with examples of the impact of energy on the creation, the Universe, environment, natural resources, and mankind. Below are verses that give us an appreciation for the miracle of the Qur'an, as it reveals information that only recently has been discovered and verified by scientists. Amazing isn't it. Just think, the Qur'an was revealed more than fourteen centuries ago, and scientists are only now beginning to make discoveries that are compatible with the revelations in the Qur'an. Therefore, the Qur'an contains information that man discovers in due time.

Iron

Thomas P. Armstrong is Emeritus Professor of Physics and Astronomy at the University of Kansas. He has worked for the National Aeronautics and Space Administration (NASA). He has worked on space investigations of the energetic charged particle environment of the Earth, interplanetary space, and the magnetospheres of Jupiter, Saturn, Neptune, and Uranus. He has developed and distributed a 23-year long data set of solar and interplanetary particle fluxes incident on the Earth's atmosphere that has provided the basis for many calculations of the atmospheric effects of solar particles. In 1995, he was interviewed by Sheikh Abdul-Majeed A. al-Zindani, of the Muslim World League in Saudi Arabia. Professor Armstrong was asked a number of questions about Qur'anic verses dealing with his field of specialization.

One of the questions asked of Professor Armstrong dealt with the following Qur'anic verse on the concept of iron:

"...We sent down iron, in which is (material for) mighty war, as well as many benefits for mankind...." (Qur'an 57:25)

Hadid is the Arabic word for iron. Professor Armstrong was asked about how iron was formed. His response was that scientists have come only recently to discover the relevant facts about the formation of the Earth. He said that the energy of the early solar system was not sufficient to produce elemental iron. In calculating the energy required to form one atom of iron, it was found to be about four times as much as the energy of the entire solar system. In other words, the entire energy of the Earth or the moon or the other planets is not sufficient to form one new atom of iron, even the energy of the entire solar system is not sufficient for that. That is why Professor Armstrong said that the scientists believe that iron is an extraterrestrial that was sent to Earth and not formed therein. Professor Armstrong concluded by stating that he *"...was impressed at how remarkably some of the ancient writings seem to correspond to modern and recent astronomy...what we have seen is remarkable, it may or may not admit of scientific explanation. There might have to be something beyond what we understand as ordinary human experience to account for the writings that we have seen."[63]*

What we can infer from Professor Armstrong's remarks is that iron was created outside of the Earth and then sent down to Earth for a purpose that is stated in the Qur'anic verse earlier quoted. Interestingly, University of Arizona scientists state they have discovered that meteorites, particularly iron meteorites, may have been critical to the evolution of life on Earth.[64] Other American scientists are of the view that iron did not form on the Earth but, rather, was carried from supernovas (catastrophic explosive death of a star resulting in an extremely bright, short-lived object that emits vast amounts of energy).[65] In his book, *Nature's Destiny*, the well-known microbiologist, Michael Denton, emphasizes the importance of iron:

"Of all the metals there is none more essential to life than iron. It is the accumulation of iron in the center of a star which triggers a supernova explosion and the subsequent scattering of the vital atoms of life throughout the cosmos...Without the iron atom, there would be no carbon-based life in the cosmos; no supernovae, no heating of the primitive earth, no atmosphere or hydrosphere. There would be no protective magnetic field, no Van Allen radiation belts, no ozone layer, no metal to make hemoglobin (in human blood), no metal to tame the reactivity of oxygen, and no oxidative metabolism."[66]

In a book entitled, *A Brief Illustrated Guide to Understanding Islam*, written by I. A. Ibrahim, it presents and highlights the scientific miracles in the Qur'an.[67] The following are excerpts from that book:

Origin of the Universe

With the aid of advanced technological equipment and methods, scientists have only recently been able to observe new stars forming out of the remnants of a cloud of *smoke*:

"Moreover He comprehended in His Design the sky, and it had been (as) smoke; He said to it and to the Earth: 'Come you together, willingly or unwillingly.' They said: 'We do come (together), in willing obedience.'" (Qur'an 41:11)

Because the Earth and the Heavens have been formed from this same *smoke*, it is evident that the Earth and the Heavens were one connected entity. Then out of this homogeneous *smoke*, they formed and separated from each other:

"Do not the unbelievers see that the Heavens and the Earth were joined together (as one Unit of Creation), before we clove them asunder? We made from water every living thing. Will they not then believe?" (Qur'an 21:30)

Deep Seas and Internal Waves

Scientists have recently discovered that there is virtually no light around a depth of 200 meters into the sea and complete darkness at a depth of about 1,000 meters. In the following verse, the Qur'an reveals what scientists are now beginning to discover with the aid of submarines and special equipment that was not available to Prophet Mohammad:

"Or (the unbelievers' state) is like the depths of darkness in a vast deep ocean, overwhelmed with billow topped by billow, topped by (dark) clouds: Depths of darkness, one above another: If a man stretches out his hand, he can hardly see it! For any to whom God giveth not light, there is no light!" (Qur'an 24:40)

The *billow* referred to is another name for wave. The deep waters of the sea are covered by waves, and above these waves are other waves, and above these waves are clouds. The first set of waves, the internal waves, cannot be seen by the naked eye; however, they can be detected by studying the temperature or salinity changes at a given location. The internal waves cover the deep waters of the sea, because the deep waters have a higher density than the waters above them. The second set of waves is on the surface of the sea, so we actually see these waves. We can also see the clouds above the second set of waves.

There is another type of miracle relative to the deep seas and internal waves. It is the story of Prophet Jonah who was swallowed up into the stomach of a large whale. Three layers of darkness enveloped Prophet Jonah: (a) darkness of the whale's stomach; (b) darkness of the bottom of the sea; and (c) darkness of the night. Prophet Jonah realized that he was imprisoned within the three layers of darkness. During the time of his imprisonment, Prophet Jonah prayed to God by repeating the invocation that he had committed a wrong (Qur'an 21:87). The wrong committed was that he had subjected himself to a seaman's traditional game of lots when faced with a storm. To lighten the load of the ship, it was decided that someone should be thrown overboard. The lots were cast three different times, and each time the lot appeared with Prophet Jonah's name. God finally forgave Prophet Jonah and had the whale eject him from its stomach onto an island (Qur'an 37:139-148).

Clouds and Lightning

The following verse in the Qur'an that states how lightning is formed:

"Seest thou not that God makes the clouds move gently, then joins them together, then makes them into a heap? – then wilt thou see rain issue forth from their midst. And He sends down from the sky mountain masses (of clouds) wherein is hail: He strikes therewith whom He pleases and He turns it away from whom He pleases. The vivid flash of His lightning well-nigh blinds the sight." (Qur'an 24:43)

Recently, meteorologists have come to know these details of cloud formation, structure, and function by using advanced equipment like planes, satellites, computers, balloons, and other equipment, to study wind and its direction, to measure humidity and its variations, and to determine the levels and variations of atmospheric pressure. Meteorologists have also found that hail, which emanates from the clouds, is a major factor in producing lightning. For example, when the hailstone comes in contact with an ice crystal, electrons flow from the colder object toward the warmer object. As a result, the hailstone becomes negatively charged and falls toward the bottom of the cloud, which also becomes negatively charged. These negative charges are then discharged as lightning.

There is another miracle mentioned in the Qur'an, i.e., the miracle of the bees. Let us examine the importance of the bee:

Energy of the Bees

"And thy Lord taught the bee to build its cells in hills, on trees, and in (men's) habitations; then to eat of all the produce (of the Earth), and find with skill the spacious paths of its Lord; there issues from within their bodies a drink of varying colours, wherein is healing for men: verily in this is a Sign for those who give thought." (Qur'an 16:68-69)

If we think about the engineering design that God created matter and energy, we find that His creation includes hexagonal shapes, for example, the habitation of bees in a beehive has units that are shaped like hexagons. The best way to build structures is to arrange the basic units comprising it in a hexagonal pattern like the following geometrical shape with numbers from 1 to 19: [68]

HEXAGON

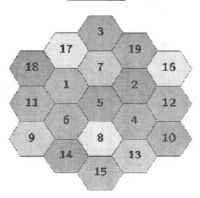

There is only one numerically linear magic hexagon. It consists of the numbers 1 to 19 so arranged that each straight line adds to the value of 38 in every direction. The value 38 is divisible by the number 19. A hexagon is a polygon that has 8 faces (6 sides + top + bottom), 18 edges (6 vertical + 6 round top + 6 round bottom), and 12 vertices (6 on top + 6 on bottom), for a total value of 38 (19*2).

It is not the beehive that is hexagonal but, rather, the honeycomb cell. The honeycomb cell is a classic example of a hexagon. A honeycomb is a mass of hexagonal wax cells built by honey bees in a beehive to contain their larva and stores of honey and pollen. First, worker bees fly out from the hive in search of nectar-rich flowers. Using its straw-like proboscis, a worker bee drinks the liquid nectar and stores it in a special stomach called the honey stomach. Within the honey stomach, enzymes break down the complex sugars of the nectar into simpler sugars, which are less prone to crystallization. With a full belly, the worker bee heads back to the hive and regurgitates the already modified nectar for a hive bee. The hive bee ingests the sugary offering and further breaks down the sugars. It then regurgitates the inverted nectar into a cell of the honeycomb. Then the hive bees beat their wings furiously, fanning the nectar to evaporate its remaining water content. As the water evaporates, the sugars thicken into honey. Once the honey is finished, the hive bee caps the beeswax cell, sealing the honey into the honeycomb for later consumption.[69]

From the time bees seek out nectar flowers to the time they form the honeycomb in a beehive hexagon, they are constantly using kinetic energy. This form of energy is best displayed by the bees flapping their wings and moving their bodies. Potential energy is stored when honeycombs are formed encasing honey for the benefit of mankind. The hexagon structure allows maximum use of each unit area in the honeycomb thereby storing more honey. While the hexagon cell structure stores maximum amount of honey, it requires a minimum amount of wax for construction. The process by which bees maneuver their way through 19 hexagons within a larger hexagon forming honeycombs is truly amazing.

According to Harun Yahya in his book, *The Miracle of the Honeybee*, the miracle of the bee lies in the ability of its brain to work at unbelievable speed. The electromagnetic energy of the bee's brain is so perfectly energized that these creatures are able to produce honey with flawless rapidity. A computer magazine, *Byte*, reported some phenomenal statistics when comparing the brain of a bee to that of a computer. While advanced computers can compute 16 billion computations per second, the brain of a bee can compute 10 trillion computations per second, or 625 times greater than that of a computer. Additionally, a bee's brain consumes less energy than a computer in performing these computations. The energy consumed by 10 million bees is the same as that used by a single 100 watt bulb. (The bee's brain consumes less than 10 microwatts of energy.) The bee is yet another proof of God's miracles.[70]

UNIVERSE, EARTH, ENVIRONMENT, AND MANKIND

CHAPTER 8

PHILOSOPHY OF ENERGY IN ISLAM

Philosophy of energy in Islam brings into focus an understanding of our existence and the components that drive that existence. What follows is a snapshot of how energy of consciousness and metaphysics plays an important role in defining our purpose in life.

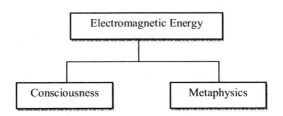

The basic foundation of life is a universal consciousness, which brings about all creation and their need for survival. All creation relates to this consciousness, which is conditioned and becomes specifically definable with individual beings and species. When personal consciousness and awareness are made subservient to the truth of everlasting consciousness, then one is in constant harmony and well-being.[71]

All forms of energy are simply different manifestations of this one consciousness, and this means that things we previously may have thought were non-living or inanimate are very much alive and connected to us. Because we are part of this consciousness, our thoughts as well as our actions can influence anything and everything in existence. Consciousness itself is a kind of energy that has intelligence and organization, which is integrally related to the tiniest of creation.[72]

Metaphysics examines the nature of reality, including the relationship between mind and matter. Metaphysics investigates principles of reality transcending those of any particular science. It is concerned with explaining the fundamental nature of being and the world.[73] Maxims and discourses on metaphysics are authored by Imam Ali Ibn Abi Talib, with particular emphasis on the concept of Unity (*Tawhid*). His discourses and sermons are considered as pivotal sources of metaphysical knowledge.[74] He was the first in Islam to open the door for logical demonstration and proof and to discuss the "divine sciences" or metaphysics (ma'arif-i ilahiyah).[75]

According to Sayed Hossein Nasr, Sayyid Muhammad H. al-Tabataba'i delved directly into the questions of metaphysics in a manner combining intellectual rigor and logical demonstration. Sayyid al-Tabataba'i discussed problems which had never appeared before in the same way among the metaphysicians of the world. Moreover, he was so energetic and devoted to metaphysics and gnosis that even in the heat of battle he would carry out intellectual discourse and discuss metaphysical questions.[76]

Consciousness

Let us first examine how energy consciousness impacts our lives.

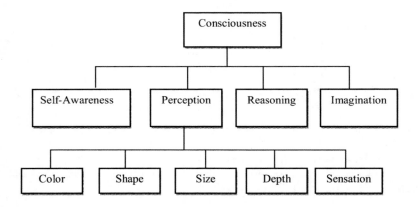

Self-Awareness

Heightened self-awareness is attained by way of energy consciousness. Self-awareness is a central aspect of any conscious mental life that consists of more than a random sequence of sensory experiences. The unity of consciousness within man helps him to perceive that God exists. Man's ability to reason provides him insight into the marvels of creation. His imagination further enhances his appreciation for the wonders God has given us. Man explores his surroundings and perceives the flawless creation as part of a perfect Cosmos. Our conscience acknowledges that the perfection of the Cosmos is the work of God. By referring to our conscience we have awareness. Awareness is achieved through wisdom, and wisdom comes about by following one's conscience. Even the cellular structure of the human body is a proof of the Creator, and wisdom and conscience helps us arrive at that conclusion.

Consciousness consists of inner, qualitative, subjective states and processes or awareness. Oversimplifying, it includes everything from feelings of love or hate, joy or sadness, comfort or anxiety, to perceiving objects visually, to making mortgage payments, to discussion on politics or economics, or to just wishing we were somewhere else.

Every conscious state has a certain qualitative feel to it. For example, the experience of tasting a soft drink is very different from hearing the sound of thunder, and both of these have a different qualitative character than the fragrance of a flower or the sighting of a rainbow. While these examples illustrate the different qualitative features of conscious experiences, they also imply subjectivity.

In order to have a qualitative feel to some extent, there must be a subject that experiences the event, because if there is no subjectivity there is no experience. While a qualitative state of conscious implies subjectivity, subjectivity implies unity. For example, if one is driving his car, he does not only see the road ahead of him but also the scenic view as well. At the same he does not just feel the pressure of his back in the driver's chair and the thoughts that run through his mind. Rather, he experiences all of these as a part of a single unified conscious field.

Perception

Perception is influenced by color, shape, size, depth, and sensation. The energy consciousness patterns reaching our senses are constantly changing, even when they come from the same object. Color, shape, and size constancy rescue us from a confusing world in which objects would seem to shrink and grow or change shape. Depth perception allows us to see three-dimensional space and to accurately judge distances. Without depth perception, we would be unable to successfully drive a car, thread a needle, or simply navigate around a room. In other words, while the perception of everything around us would appear to be flat, the reality is that nothing is really flat but curved.

Perception organizes our sensations so we can accurately visualize our environment and its surroundings. This is accomplished by the brain actively selecting, organizing, and integrating sensory information.

The unity of consciousness means to be aware of a number of things at the same time. It is a group of representations being related to one another such that to be conscious of any of them is to be conscious of others as a single group. The concept of intention in Islam is a form of consciousness. For example, it is our intention to face the *qiblah* (direction of prayer) when praying. Here our conscious state has both a qualitative and a subjective effect. As we face the *qiblah* in prayer and supplication, we feel and experience a sense of unification within ourselves. This unified feeling is heightened as we perform our group prayers together. As there is only one *qiblah*, it is the pivotal point that unites the entire Muslim *Ummah* (community) and brings into harmony the feelings of Muslims. It is the point at which the emotions of Muslims converge. It is the axis at which the feelings of mercy and unity are interconnected.

Reasoning

Muslims need to restore the unity by eradicating the seeds of ignorance, which have paralyzed the human consciousness. This paralysis has afflicted both their steadfastness and their vital intellectual behavior. How we overcome this paralysis is by understanding the causes of this intellectual dilemma and remedying the logic by sound reflection and contemplation. The connection between logic and education must be restored. While reasoning is encouraged, it must be within the aegis of Islamic principles. These principles are manifested in the Qur'an, which guides the Muslim *Ummah* as to the proper course in achieving harmony within the conscious mind. Islam encourages reasoning, thought, logic, and personal opinion. It is this flexibility in having differences of opinion that underscores the meaning of God's Mercy. As Muslims, we seek to understand and explore the secrets of nature and of the creation. We explore nature's beauty and symmetry as well as harmony. Islam is universal and comprehensive.

Imagination

Conscious Muslims are responsible for developing a firm and secure foundation for the restoration of the unity of the *Ummah*, and ultimately rebuilding the nation of Islam. Imagination is a vital element in building a better future. The Muslim leadership must imagine and promote a more sustainable unity of Muslim brotherhood and solidarity, if they are going to enlist the Muslim community to join. But how to harness each other's imagination is vital to attaining the unity, and Muslims achieve this by starting to liberate their own.

Each day of our lives we are influenced by our consciousness. No one is exempt from having consciousness. However, some people can control their consciousness better than others. Let us look at ourselves from the viewpoint of energy consciousness. Our physical world is replete with energy. The process of creating energy consciousness may be likened to the way a driver revs the engine of his automobile. As the rate of revving is increased, sound energy waves resonate from the amplitudes and frequencies that collaborate with each other. Of course, the result is a loud noise that is quite disturbing to the ears. Whether it is a driver revving his engine to create sound patterns or a maestro waving his wand to blend in the music of his musicians, it takes a high degree of energy consciousness, commitment and practice.

Consciousness is like the sound of an engine or the sound of music, i.e., a continuous arrangement of life energy. Like the automobile driver or the maestro, we also have an inherent need to advance our competence to create consciousness. However, consciousness is not the same for everyone. During our lifetime, our consciousness will not always be the same. In other words, the energy consciousness of activities in our life varies, as they are complex and contain many distinct lines of energy. As a result, each of these distinct lines of energy represents the distinct human attitude that created it. The mind imagines and interprets these distinct lines of energy and acts accordingly. How to harness this energy consciousness in order to control and influence the dynamics of these distinct lines of energy can help generate self-fulfillment in our lives.

Energy Force

The consciousness energy force has an effect on each and every moment in our lives, whether the effect is conscious, subconscious, or unconscious. The energy that we attach ourselves to in our lives is a conscious choice for us. It is energy that helps create a balance or imbalance within our body and mind. For every thought, emotion, action, and belief within our physical world, there is an electromagnetic stream of energy. By opening our minds to a higher level of energy consciousness, we attach our minds to that energy source. Our thoughts and actions will image that energy source. Each and every energy source will intersect with other energy sources in the same manner that highways intersect with each other. We will not follow just one energy highway, but we will travel down many energy streams. Because of the frequent intersection of energy, we will always have alternative choices to make during our lifetime.

If we choose to attach ourselves to an energy consciousness of victimization, we will allow that energy force to course though our bodies. If we choose to attach ourselves to the material, egotistical energy consciousness, our entire world will be focused on the concept of collecting material things within our world. If we choose to attach ourselves to a service energy source, we will dedicate our lives to helping others. If we attach ourselves to the energy source of hate, anger, and fear, we will live a life of hate, anger, and fear.

The spiritual definition of energy is an electromagnetic energy force with constant movement and change. Energy must indeed move; it has no alternative. In the essence of this movement is interpenetration and interweaving. Each movement creates because it, too, is energy. Therefore, all of life is interrelated, interpenetrated, and interwoven. Each thought, each word, and each action creates an electromagnetic energy force on all other thoughts, words, and actions. It is our mind that envisions, imagines, dreams, creates, and knows. It is our mind that focuses the power of creation for our consciousness to see and to understand. [77]

111

Metaphysics

Generally, metaphysics can be categorized with the nature of the (a) universe (cosmology); (b) existence (ontology); and (c) knowledge (epistemology). Cosmology, ontology, and epistemology are interconnected, as each influences the other. Cosmology is the study of the experience of the Universe. Ontology is the study of being. Epistemology is the division of philosophy that investigates the nature and origin of knowledge. Let us explore the larger reality of consciousness within the metaphysical disciplines of cosmology, ontology, and epistemology. Simply, cosmology deals with where it came from, while ontology deals with what is there, and epistemology deals with how we know it.

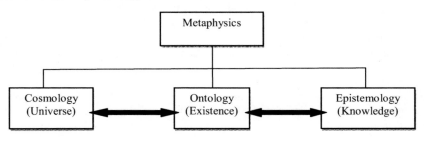

Cosmology

The Cosmos is a complex and orderly system, such as our Universe. It is a well-ordered and unified system that is perfect in order and arrangement. In Islam, the concept of the Cosmos is one whereby there is movement in all that exists, and that this movement continues to advance until Judgment Day when the Cosmos is transformed into a new creation.

There is unity within the Cosmos. Everything in nature follows an orderly design. There is consistency and harmony in the marvels of nature, for example the growth and decay of plants and animals. For this to happen, nature has to be created and planned. This plan entails a comprehensive design that has to be conceived from intelligence beyond our comprehension. Therefore, the Cosmos was created by an eternal existence, an existence that always was and always will be forever as God.

Cosmologists, or scientists who study the Universe, adamantly state that in the beginning the whole Universe was just a cloud of smoke. The Qur'an reveals the following verse:

"Moreover He comprehended in His Design the sky, and it had been as smoke: He said to it and to the Earth: 'Come you together, willingly or unwillingly.' They said: 'We do come together, in willing obedience.'" (Qur'an 41:11)

Since the Earth and the Heavens were shaped from this single smoke, then they must have been linked together as one entity. Again, the Qur'an gives us the answer:

"Do not the unbelievers see that the Heavens and the Earth were joined together as one unity of creation, before we clove them asunder? We made from water every living thing. Will they not then believe?" (Qur'an 21:30)

How could Prophet Mohammad have known this to be so when, in fact, cosmology in his time was in its infant stage? This is a miracle of the Qur'an, the Ultimate Revelation of God. In pre-Islam, ignorance prevailed. At that time, illiteracy was the norm, and education was reserved for the privileged few. The Qur'an was revealed, and the wonders of creation were illustrated. During the Age of Ignorance, creative and innovative thoughts were virtually non-existent, and no one was able to scientifically perceive and understand the mysteries of the enormous Cosmos. The Qur'an changed all that, as it discloses facts that only the Creator of the Cosmos could know. In Islam, the Universe is not static. God is steadily expanding the Universe, and again the Qur'an gives the explanation:

"And among His Signs is the creation of the Heavens and the Earth, and the living creatures that He Has scattered through them: and He Has Power to gather them together when He Wills." (Qur'an 42:29)

"(He) Who created thee, and fashioned thee in due proportion; in whatever form He wills, does He put thee together." (Qur'an 82:7-8)

"While indeed He created you through regular stages. See you not how God created the seven heavens one above another? And made the moon a light in their midst, and made the sun as a lamp." (Qur'an 71:14-16)

This means that life, in whatever form, is scattered throughout the Universe. This means that life in some form or other exists in the galaxies. This Universe is an entity that was created and sustained by God. It is God Who created man, so that man can harvest the land and seek out knowledge and meaning to his existence. Towards this end, God made the Earth and the Heavens submissive to man. God gave man a free will in order for man to be responsible for his actions. It is this free will that gives meaning to humanity, and the concept of reward and punishment in the Hereafter manifests itself in the accountability of man's actions on Earth. To attain ultimate bliss, man must live a life of virtues such as piety and knowledge. As man's knowledge expands, he sees more and more how unity is dominant in the Cosmos. In his progress, man's role is a perpetual quest for knowledge. It is in this manner that we must constantly seek God's Benevolence and Mercy and to remember God as we submit our will to the Will of God.

113

How man increases his understanding of the unity in the Cosmos is by obtaining more knowledge and wisdom about the physical world:

- Impact of the moon on the ocean tides.
- Affect of the Earth's magnetic field on the migration of birds.
- Harmony in solar system as caused by gravitational and centrifugal forces.

In reality, the unity of creation continues to exist allowing for multiple forms of creation to maintain their linkage to the initial *"Oneness"* of the Universe. The Qur'an points to the continued expansion of the Universe:

"With power and skill We constructed the Firmament: for it is We Who create the vastness of Space. And We have spread out the (spacious) Earth: how excellently We do spread out! And of everything We have created pairs: that you may receive instruction." (Qur'an 51:47-49)

Even the structure of the Universe is consistent with modern scientific findings:

"He Who created the seven Heavens one above another...." (Qur'an 67:3)

In addition, the linkage of the speed of light with the concept of relativity is yet another example of the unity of the Cosmos. The premise here is that time is not absolute in the Universe:

"He rules (all) affairs from the Heavens to the Earth: in the end (all affairs) will go up to Him, on a Day, the space whereof will be (as) a thousand years of reckoning." (Qur'an 32:5)

There is integration of nature's phenomena within Islam. This integration helps reinforce and strengthen our lives, whether spiritual or moral, political or economic, social or cultural. Each of these aspects is uniquely integrated, as they do not separate from one another. In balanced form, these aspects fit and flow with the nature of man. Humanity is interconnected with natural phenomena, as it is located at the center of the Cosmos. This interaction of human life within the Cosmos is the channel by which light enters the world of nature.

We see ourselves reflected in nature, as we penetrate into nature's inner meaning by probing into our own inner depths. Despair within us can lead to disorder, while harmony can bring about the best in character. What brings about the unity within us is Islam. It is Islam that is the universal order, for it affords us the vehicle by which to gain peace and happiness. By submitting our will to the Will of God, Islam brings us into harmony with nature.

According to Islam, it is Divine Guidance that is the only source of knowledge. The Cosmos is a moral order, and the unity of mankind is that which reflects the essence of spirituality and piety. Our knowledge of unity leads us to understand its process, i.e., Unity of

114

God, Unity of the Cosmos, Unity of Creation, and Unity of Purpose. In essence, Islam means conformity to the natural law.

As the Universe is a Cosmos, everything in nature follows a carefully structured and precise balanced order. There is a consistent order or reliability and permanence of laws governing the mechanism of the Universe. God created everything in the Universe with a perfect plan. The Qur'an reveals that there are Signs of God in the natural world, such as its balances and the rhythms of life. Some of these are the cycles of life and death, the seasons of the year, the orbits of the planets, and the mysteries of the human body. This perfect order and balance are neither haphazard nor accidental. This order and balance extend to how humans should relate to their natural world.

Humans are an integral part of the natural world and as such they should fulfill its needs without being indulged in its desires. For example, humans should not pollute the environment or destroy plants or kill animals for sport. Rather they should respect the natural milieu and take from it only that which is needed to sustain their lives. Islam encourages us to discover and observe the natural world as Signs that point to God. God has given mankind the capacity to reason. As we reason, we realize that the natural order works because it is in submission to God.

Ontology

Ontology deals with questions concerning which entities exist or can be said to exist, and how such entities can be grouped, related within a hierarchy, and subdivided according to similarities and differences. God sustains all existence by His Will. God alone created the Universe, and all manifestations are witness to His Divine Will.

Nothing comes to existence by chance, and nobody creates himself or anybody else. Life is given to man by God, and He is the only Rightful One to take it back; no one else has the right to destroy a life without His permission. God helps man to fulfill the purpose of life and realize the goal of existence. Life is a trust from God. Man is a trustee who should use his trust with honesty and skill, and be mindful of God with consciousness of responsibility to Him. Islam has laid down a complete system of regulations and principles to show man how to live it, what to take and what to leave, and what to do and what to avoid. In Islam, man's entire individual and social life is an exercise in developing and strengthening his relationship with God.[78]

The existence of nearly all life on Earth is fueled by light from the sun. Without the energy given off by our sun, life would cease to exist. Sunlight gives the necessary energy so that plants can grow, which produces the oxygen that is essential to our survival. We need energy to power us just like any other machine, and this comes from the food that we eat and the oxygen we breathe. Humans need to collect and expend energy to maintain their Earthly existence. The human body is indeed an aerial that can transmit and receive energy. In other words, human existence strongly depends on the energy flow supporting the life on our planet.

The human energy field is always receiving energy from the Universe, as this energy sustains our existence.

Basically, there are four elements of human existence: (a) physical elements; (b) elements of the senses; (c) power elements; and (d) spiritual elements. These elements intertwine with the body (prime matter) and soul (substantial form). The physical elements are comprised of earth, air, fire, and water. The elements of the senses are sight, sound, touch, taste, and smell. The power elements consist of the intellect, anger, passion, and imagination. The spiritual elements are faith, prayer, fasting, charity, pilgrimage, struggle, ethics, and beliefs. In addition, every deed that we do in the way of good draws us closer to God. As long as our intention is pure, even if we obtain some material benefit from the good deed, it is acceptable to God.

Physical sustenance is a blessing. God provides us with light and rain as well as food, drink, and the senses. When we speak about feeling energy in metaphysics we are speaking about using our senses. All living things are made up of atoms, molecules, and cells, which generate electromagnetic energy that we are able to sense. For example, we may witness a quarrel between two individuals. We can feel the electromagnetic energy of that tension resonate through our human system, even though we may not have knowledge of what caused that quarrel.

Moral substance, likewise, is a blessing. God provided us with Prophets to teach us spiritual well-being and the concepts of Islam. These blessings should not be taken for granted or abused. We need to practice self-restraint (*sabr*) relative to these blessings. We must be grateful to God for bestowing upon us such favors. Life is from God and death is from God:

"...It is He Who gives life and death...." (Qur'an 57:2)

God's Blessing transcends the concepts of life, death, partition (*barzagh*), resurrection, and eternity. Man is an everlasting being, and death is only a step towards this eternal life. The eternal future rests on the deeds and actions of one's stay in the Earthly existence. Man has the free will to choose his path in life. How well he chooses decides his outcome. Death is the separation of the soul from the physical body. That soul travels to a partition (*barzagh*) in which it becomes more aware of the facts of existence. This partition lies between the present life and the resurrection. In the resurrection every soul shall be given a visible body. Now everyone becomes perfectly aware of the existence of God. Our existence is dependent on the Will of God. Birth and rebirth are two distinct blessings (*ni'ma*) of a first and second creation.

Epistemology

Epistemology deals with knowledge, which may be obtained through proverbs, folktales, music, dance, rituals, symbols, metaphors, etc. Knowledge comes to us innately through ideas as well as through our senses. In other words, we know because we perceive it. Two spheres intersect to describe what we know – the sphere of truth and the sphere of belief. Knowledge lies between these two spheres relative to how we acquire knowledge and we know what we know. Generally, epistemology deals with the means of production of knowledge, as well as skepticism about different knowledge claims. Epistemology primarily addresses the questions of (a) what is knowledge; (b) how is knowledge acquired; (c) who do people know; and (d) how do we know what we know.

Energy is the fuel of life. The more fuel we have the more we can accomplish in life. Likewise, energy fuels our capacity to think and know. On the other hand, it is knowledge that can enable us to harness energy to be used effectively and efficiently. For example, our lifestyles can be a factor in depleting energy resources. We need knowledge to learn how to avoid wasting both internal and external energies. We can be energized through our minds, for example, generating new ideas that derive from knowledge.

The only way to attain happiness is through knowledge. Muslims consider knowledge to be the grasping of the immaterial forms, natures, essences, or realities of things. The forms of things are either material (existing in matter) or immaterial (existing in themselves). Once in the mind, the pure forms act as the pillars of knowledge. The mind constructs objects from these forms, and with these objects it makes judgments. Logic is the key to the knowledge of the natures of things, and this knowledge is the key to happiness. Muslims believe that above the senses is the rational soul, which consists of the practical intellect and the theoretical intellect. The theoretical intellect is responsible for knowledge. The practical knowledge concerns itself only with the proper management of the body through apprehension of particular things so that it can do the good and avoid the bad.[79]

Relative to the intellect, al-Farabi (872 AD – 950 AD), an Islamic philosopher, states the following in his *Risala fi'l-Aql*:

"The lowest stage of existence for man is that in which, in order to subsist, he needs the body as the form needs matter. His next higher state of existence is that in which he does not depend for subsistence on the body as matter; nevertheless, he needs for all his actions or for most of them some powers of his body and is positively benefited by them...The highest state of existence is attained by man when his actions are not in anything other than himself; that is when he masters his whole energy to realize his innermost self as a result of which his being and action and whatever he does become one and the same...."[80]

117

Attaining self-actualization occurs when the potential intellect transforms into the actual intellect. When this happens, the actual intellect knows itself, and its existence is separate from matter. Here, the actual intellect becomes the acquired intellect, which is the highest level that the intellect can reach. What al-Farabi believes is that the active intellect is a separate form that never existed and never will exist in matter. The advancing of knowledge will purify the soul thereby elevating and perfecting man's intellect.[81] In other words, the potential intellect has the capacity to be actual and thus perfect. We can attain self-actualization, for example, patience (*sabr*), via the vehicle of knowledge, which makes the intellect disengage itself from matter. Self-actualization becomes a reality when the active intellect and acquired intellect unite.

Knowledge is the panacea for overcoming ignorance. By seeking knowledge we are enlightened. Knowledge is not only a cure for ignorance, but it also guides us. The Book of Knowledge is the Qur'an, which enlightens us and provides the guidance in our daily lives. Undoubtedly, those who have knowledge of God are not equal to those who do not. Those who have knowledge are conscious of the truth and have a favorable influence on those with whom they come in contact. In contrast, those who are ignorant muddle through their lives, unsuccessfully trying to gratify their desires. In short, the ignorant fail to gain consciousness of their purpose and duty in this life.

For Muslims, knowledge is a means to an end. When God created us from the wombs of our mothers, we were ignorant. God gave us the senses of hearing and sight and of touch and smell as well as of taste. Through these senses we are able to acquire knowledge. Whether we acquire knowledge from reading or hearing the Qur'an or whether we witness the marvels of creation, it is through these senses that we are able to function. God has provided us with the sources of knowledge, two of which are His Creation and His Revelation. Prophet Mohammad said:

"Seek knowledge from the cradle to the grave." (Sahih al-Bukhari))

Even worship is manifested through knowledge. We increase our faith via Islamic knowledge. Believers constantly seek knowledge in order to increase their faith and direct their course to the straight path. Each time a believer searches for knowledge, he will have driven further on the path to Paradise. Seeking knowledge is part of our faith, as it helps us get a clear perception about our origin, our purpose, and our way of life. Knowledge becomes the lamp that illuminates the soul and brings about happiness. There is a great difference between those who seek knowledge and those who wish to remain ignorant. Those who seek knowledge learn the truth and obtain insight, while the ignorant remain blind trekking the path of Satan.

Islamic knowledge is acquired in many ways. For example, we are encouraged to explore and study the Qur'an and the Hadiths (Traditions), which provide the bases for Islamic knowledge. Listening to a *khutbah* (sermon) and reading a scholarly Islamic article or book are other means of acquiring knowledge. When seeking Islamic knowledge, we ought to make our intention (*niyyah*) to spend time to understand it and to plan our daily lives around it. Seeking knowledge provides us with the necessity to teach others about Islam. Intention drives the action, and God looks favorably upon those whose intention is to acquire and spread knowledge for His sake.

Knowledge is vital in understanding from whence we came and to where we are going. How we conduct our daily lives is based on knowledge of Islam and what Islam asks of us. Therefore, it is apparent that to self-actualize as Muslims in our daily lives, we need to increase our knowledge and understanding of Islam. In addition, as we increase our knowledge we must also put it to practice. Faith and knowledge without practice is insignificant. Always knowledge should be sought for the purpose of obtaining God's Pleasure. The capacity of knowledge is God's Gift, which, when exercised, will lead the individual to a deeper knowledge of himself and the wonders of creation. What is important is that as knowledge leads to serving the Islamic society, it also gives life and strength to that society.

There is a great deal of truth in the adage that knowledge is freedom and ignorance is slavery. Human freedom cannot and does not rely on ignorance and randomness. Human freedom is the capacity to make choices based on reasons, and this expands with knowledge. The best way to combat ignorance is to heighten our struggle (*jihad*) against our ego, the major barrier to clear thinking. The struggle against ignorance requires that we continue to escalate our understanding of Islam, which provides the prescription for dealing with social issues including ethnic conflicts, religious and cultural differences, poverty, ethics and moral values.

The struggle against ignorance is one of the most important struggles we will ever fight and a struggle that we ultimately must win, if Islam as we know it is to survive. Winning the struggle against ignorance will require leaders with great knowledge and wisdom who understand the dilemma we face. Winning the struggle against ignorance represents a major challenge. The issues facing us today are far more difficult and complex than they ever have been before, and the stakes are getting progressively higher. Knowledge is indeed power. The less we know, the less we can contribute. We have a major job ahead of us to ensure that education becomes our number one priority and that we ultimately are victorious in the struggle against ignorance.

Ethics of Energy in Islam

Ibn Miskawayh (932 AD – 1030 AD, was an Islamic philosopher who specialized in the study of morals. His most important and influential work was *Tahdhib al-Akhlaq (Ethical Instruction)*, which dealt with the science of ethics consisting of six discourses: The Principles of Ethics, Character and Its Refinement, The Good and Its Division, Justice, Love and Friendship, and The Health of the Soul. His premise is that man attempts to attain spiritual perfection until he reaches the "pure Divine virtue." However, man has both the pleasures of the senses as well as of the mind. "The man who is truly happy is the one whose pleasures are natural and not abnormal, mental and not sensory, genuine and not emotional, Divine and not carnal." The cause of this happiness is wisdom, as a "reflection of health upon the soul."[82] Miskawayh's book provides insight into the ethics of energy, and his discourse paved the way for scholars to further study the many facets of morality both from the standpoint of the nature of man as well as the nature of our environment.

Ethics of energy covers a wide spectrum of balance ranging from safeguarding the environment, protecting our bodies, conserving natural resources, and governing justice and morality in the society. From an Islamic perspective, this balance necessitates that the ethical aspects of energy are imbedded in an understanding that God, not we, created the Earth. Therefore, we cannot do with the Earth as we please but, rather, protect what God has given us. As trustees, we have a responsibility to care for the Earth and keep it in balance with all that God has given us.

There are many issues relative to the ethical aspects of energy and their implications on the environment and mankind. The environmental consequences of energy production, distribution, and consumption invite consideration of the ethical implications of both practice and policy. What are our ethical obligations to manage the Earth's resources and natural environment in a sustainable manner? How should these obligations be enacted, institutionalized, and implemented?

Issues dealing with human values are in the realm of ethics and philosophy. From the standpoint of the human body, the ethics of maintaining and sustaining a healthy energy field requires us to be responsive. As the human body functions on the basis of energy, it cannot exist without a constant supply of new energy. In other words, energy is interwoven and interconnected with every cell and movement in our bodies. Energy is the lifeblood of our bodies and plays an essential role in sustaining our life on Earth. The overall purpose of ethics is to guide us so that body and mind are in balance with our energy field. What we do with our human energy fields requires self-accountability. It is self-accountability that is the cornerstone of ethics.

Knowledge of ethics helps us cleanse our body, mind and soul. As a positive energy force, knowledge of ethics can be the panacea for erasing bad thoughts or vices from our mind. This type of knowledge energizes and purifies our body, mind and soul with moral qualities that heighten our Islamic personality. We should constantly seek guidance from the knowledge of ethics in order to become better Muslims.

While morality is a major source of strength of the Islamic personality, immorality is a major cause of weakness. Morality is a key to harmony and balance within our energy field as well as within the society. Islam is a comprehensive way of life, and morality is one of the cornerstones of Islam. Moral conduct is the essence of virtues. All Prophets attained self-actualization in virtues, as their personalities were molded and immersed with moral conduct.

Introspection and self-assessment heightens our ethical consciousness. In order for our human energy field to generate positive energy, we need to follow a code of ethics and act accordingly. Fasting is a code of ethics, as it elicits positive energy by ridding our bodies of toxic substances. Another example of a code of ethics is to exert our energy towards maintaining peace and justice in the society. A code of ethics ensures that reasoned and ethical action is a sign of a civilized society. Ethics includes the ideas of fairness, justice, equality, and compassion. What is needed is a more ethical approach to the environment to sustain its survival and our own.

Energy and Patience (*Sabr*)

Many of us go through life wanting to understand more clearly our metaphysical relationship with God. In search of knowledge and wisdom, we broaden our horizons and equip ourselves with the tools to help fulfill this mission. As we strive towards self-actualization, we find ourselves thirsty and eager to learn even more about Islam. From time to time we deter from that cause by falling prey to the desires and evils of this world. Lack of education in Islam keeps us short of ever self-actualizing ourselves as complete Muslims. What is needed is a mechanism by which we can be assured that our faith will be complete and secure. The mechanism needed to bind the tie between the ideological aspects (Articles of Faith) and practical aspects (Branches of Faith) of Islam is patience (*sabr*).

Patience becomes one of the most important aspects in our daily lives. In short, patience transcends into what we call *taqwah* (consciousness of God). Thereafter, everything we do is *kurbatan ilallah*, that is, to become nearer to God. Like a ship lost at sea, we may not know which direction to turn. Patience helps us find that direction, as it is not only a serious search but also the energy to assist us in reaching that destination. Patience energizes our spiritual drive so that we can have a deeper understanding of our duties and Islamic obligations. The energy of patience is the light that steers us to the right path.

In Islam, effort is attained through patience. This effort is not automatic; rather, it takes a great deal of concentration, energy, and control of one's inner self. We must strive in the way of Islam, and that way is achieved through a concerted and genuine effort by each of us. While faith is a requisite for prayer, patience is a requisite for faith:

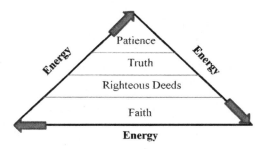

Faith alone is not enough. Faith and prayer are justified when we worship and submit to God alone. This is accomplished by being steadfast and patient. To merely pray, for example, without steadfastness and self-restraint in prayer weakens the person's resolve. With effort, patience strengthens our prayer. While faith and patience complement each other, they are reinforced and strengthened by righteous deeds and truth. With patience, one quietly performs his righteous deed and seeks his only reward from the good in having performed that deed. Reaching the highest level of certainty, the certainty of truth, one must have the patience and capacity to receive and understand the truth, be free of sin, be free of worldly interests, and be free of prejudice.

Patience needs a spark to elicit it within ourselves. Just as a battery needs a charge to run a machine, patience needs an electrical charge to make it surface and function. Electrolytes (special minerals that create polarity for the cells) help channel the correct electric potential between nerve cells that enable the transmission of nerve signals to arouse one's patience. Electrolytes conduct electricity and are found in the body fluid, tissue, and blood, for example, magnesium, sodium, and potassium. Proper balance is essential for muscle coordination, heart function, fluid absorption and excretion, nerve function, and concentration. Patience takes a great deal of concentration to emerge. When electrolytes are depleted, one's concentration may feel like it's running on half-power. When this happens, patience will respond sluggishly and an overall sense of fatigue and weakness will triumph over stamina and endurance.

It is not easy to be patient and steadfast. It requires a great deal of concentration. This concentration consumes a great deal of energy. As we strive to overcome our human weakness, we may fall prey to our ego and lose not only our concentration but consciousness as well. By only being patient and steadfast can we sustain our inner strength and energy to persevere, i.e., to have the will power to overcome temptations. Patience is the vehicle by which we can conquer this type of negative energy. Having patience is letting go of our negative energy. Patience strengthens the will and the power of perseverance to overcome hardship, calamity, and adversity.

Patience is like electromagnetic energy. When we are spiritually enlightened, we gain energy. When we are lethargic and depressed, we lose energy. Patience with knowledge enlightens us and provides the resolution to change our condition and improve our well-being. The source of light is energy, and the outcome of patience radiates from that energy. Patience has two sides – positive and negative. Positive patience helps us in times of struggle or strife, while negative patience weakens our spirituality and makes us lose sight of our Islamic duties and obligations. In times of misfortune and hardship, God causes a light to descend upon the hearts of those He loves by strengthening them with great serenity. By building our energy of patience and steadfastness, we are better prepared to pass God's test by following His Commands.

TRANSFER OF LEADERSHIP
DIVINE ENERGY

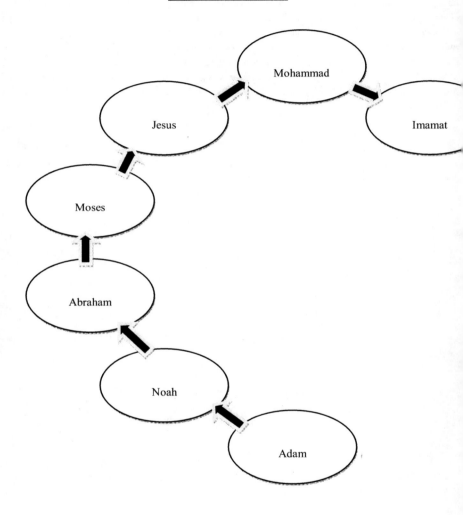

CHAPTER 9

MANIFESTATION OF ENERGY: PROPHET MOHAMMAD AND IMAM ALI IBN ABI TALIB

Prophets

All the Prophets had a role to perform, and the foundation of their mission was to preach Divine Unity. All the Prophets concentrated on the basic principle, as stated in the Qur'an:

"Verily, this Brotherhood of yours is a single Brotherhood, and I am your Lord and Cherisher: therefore, serve Me (and no other)." (Qur'an 21:92)

Many Prophets were sent to convey this message of Oneness to the people. While many Prophets came at different times in the course of history, they all agreed on a single premise, which is that God is One. The summation of their spiritual works became fully realized with the Final Revelation – the Qur'an. There are twenty-five Prophets listed by name in the Qur'an of which five are Messengers. Each of the five Messengers (Noah, Abraham, Moses, Jesus, and Mohammad) delivered the Message of God. They delivered to mankind the spiritual works by which we can perform good deeds. There were many other Prophets whose names were not cited in the Qur'an, but are alluded to.

God alone decided who is to be a Prophet. What distinguishes a Prophet from others is that he performs miracles and is infallible. The Qur'an is replete with revelation of miracles performed by Prophets. For example, the miracle of Noah surviving *The Deluge* with his Ark; or the miracle of Abraham walking in an extremely scorching fire untouched; or the miracle of Prophet Moses who turned a staff into a serpent; or the miracle of Prophet Jesus who spoke from the cradle and also brought the dead back to life; or the greatest miracle of all whereby Prophet Mohammad delivered to mankind the Qur'an. And each of these miracles is covered in the Qur'an with precision and depth. These Prophets had an energy that transcended human energy; it was a creative energy. When performing a miracle, the creative energy of each of these Prophets enabled them to establish the supremacy and authenticity of their arguments.

The Qur'an is replete with stories of many Prophets and of Mary. The mother of Prophet Jesus is the only female mentioned by name in the Qur'an, and a chapter is named in her honor. Each Prophet mentioned in the Qur'an had a purpose, whether it was to address the ills of the society, oppression and tyranny, disbelievers, or a moral condition. Each Prophet was sent by God to guide mankind. Some of the Prophets had greater responsibility and importance, thereby being called Major Prophets. All the messages focused on the One God and the unity of brotherhood. Each Prophet was gifted with a kind of supernatural power or creative energy by means of which he worked one or more miracles to prove his credibility as a Prophet.

As each Prophet performed miracles, each was also infallible or incapable of committing sin. They were immune to sin. As they were free and protected from error, they were also unyielding to error and sin. In addition, they were gifted with great intellectual and supernatural powers and revelation as well as perfect moral virtues. The lifestyle of each Prophet is the direct result of Divine teachings and guidance. Each Prophet was the continuation of the Prophet that preceded him, except for Adam who was the first Prophet. This continuation is like a rope extended with each knot representing a Prophet. As the Qur'an is often referred to as the *Rope of God*, then each of God's Messengers provides a certain strength and intensity to that *Rope*.

The transfer of creative energy transcended through the ages, beginning with Adam, followed by the multitude of Prophets, five of whom were enlightened and radiated as God's Messengers: Noah, Abraham, Moses, Jesus, and Mohammad, the Seal of the Prophets. Prophet Mohammad then, by the Grace and Divine Will of God, transferred the leadership of Islam to the Imamat, beginning with Imam Ali Ibn Abi Talib. The Prophets, Messengers, and Imamat were genuinely inspired by God, as they are the sources of light and creative energy that carried out and fulfilled the Creator's Divine Plan. These Messengers and Imamat personified the character, personality, and disposition of flawlessness, submission, and devotion. They were gifted with knowledge and armored with courage to convey to humanity the importance of faith, righteous deeds, truth, and patience.

The miracle for the Imamat was their knowledge, qualifications, and conduct that, by the Grace of God, was molded in perfection and inherited from the lineage of Prophet Mohammad. Prophet Mohammad and the Imamat have illuminated our spirits, as their energy flows through every facet of our soul, body, and mind. As heirs of this energy, we must own up to our responsibility to be the guardians and trustees of the faith of Islam. We must instill this radiant energy within our children, so they can carry on the legacy of Islam. Following is a discussion of Prophet Mohammad and the example of how God enlightened him with a superhuman and creative energy.

The Night Journey of the Ascent (Isra' and Mi'raj) of Prophet Mohammad

Never in the history of mankind has the light of divine energy been so completely manifested, demonstrated, and fulfilled than in Prophet Mohammad. He was molded and refined in the spirituality of Islam:

- Purification and enlightenment of the soul, body, and mind.

- Awareness and self-realization of God.

- Revelation of the Qur'an.

- Night Journey of the Ascent (Isra' and Mi'raj) following the sequence of experiences.

- Manifestation of Prophet's purpose and resolve.

- Vision of spiritual and cultural transformation of the society.

- Establishment of a system of ethics, virtues, and justice.

- Transfer of power and leadership to the Imamat.

"Glory to (God) Who did take His servant for a Journey by night from the Sacred Mosque (Mecca) to the Farthest Mosque (Jerusalem) whose precincts We did bless, - in order that We might show him some of Our Signs: for He is the One Who heareth and seeth (all things)." (17:1; Qur'an)

"Will you then dispute with him concerning what he saw? For indeed he saw him (Gabriel) at another ascent, near the Lote-tree beyond which none may pass: near it is the Garden of Abode. Behold, the Lote-tree was shrouded (in mystery unspeakable!) His sight never swerved, nor did it go wrong. Indeed he did see of the Greatest Signs of his Lord." (53:12-18; Qur'an)

Prophet Mohammad was the vehicle by which the universality of divine energy was to be transformed into the minds of not only the inhabitants of the Arabian Peninsula but to all of mankind. He was the mercy to all humanity, not just the Muslims. The Night Journey of the Ascent (Isra' and Mi'raj) was the crowning touch of divine inspiration, as Prophet Mohammad self-actualized in complete awareness of the Creator and His Divine Plan. Prophet Mohammad's mission was to awaken the unconscious minds of all humanity. The Ascent gave rise to the formation of a new culture, a new order of things, which transcended beyond the provinciality and tribal way of living prevalent at that time.

In order to bring about change in the society, Prophet Mohammad had to be equipped with superhuman energy. The behavior of the community was ingrained in their lifestyles that were virtually impossible to change. It was a tall order for Prophet Mohammad, but God had prepared him well, and the Ascent reinforced all the means by which to succeed. He transcended the limitations of the human mind to bring about a code of ethics, justice, and tolerance. It was the Ascent that gave Mohammad the conviction, self-assurance, and wisdom to undertake this challenge and change, i.e., the transformation from a pagan society to a faith-driven Islamic community. He was the liaison between Heaven and Earth bringing the Qur'an to enlighten mankind.

In his book, *Me'raj - the Night Ascension*, Mullah Faidh al Kashani, gives a thorough explanation of Prophet Mohammad's Night Journey of Isra' and Mi'raj. The treatise of the *Me'raj – the Night Ascension*, according to the narrations of Faidh al Kashani, is a collection of traditions taken from the speech of Imam Ja'far as-Sadiq.[83]

During the first part of the Night Journey, with the aid of a steed named al-Buraq, Archangel Gabriel took Prophet Mohammad from the Sacred Mosque in Mecca to the site of the *Farthest Mosque*, al-Aqsa Mosque, in Jerusalem. The meaning of al-Buraq is lightning, and God exhibits how He can have a steed made of light, unlike the normal light that obeys the laws of relativity, travel much faster than the speed of normal light. He disembarked at this place and visited various places – including Bait al-Laham, the birthplace of Jesus. At the al-Aqsa Mosque, he met with earlier Prophets, such as Abraham, Moses, and Jesus. Prophet Mohammad led the prayer that included these Prophets and Gabriel.

On the second part of the Night Journey, Gabriel took Prophet Mohammad to the Heavens where he witnessed the celestial bodies and the entire Universe. The Night Journey was completed in a very short period of time during the night. Prophet Mohammad saw Paradise and Hell and was enlightened by the wonders of creation and existence. The Greatest Signs of God were revealed by the Creator to Prophet Mohammad who fully understood the supreme omnipotent power of God. Prophet Mohammad then journeyed to a region known as Sidratul' Muntaha, a place covered in grandeur and magnificence. It was from this same path that he traversed that he returned home. It is important to note that the Night Journey of Prophet Mohammad was both bodily and spiritually. The Night Journey was the culmination and fulfillment of perfection of mankind's religious development.

Touring the various dimensions of the Seven Heavens, only Prophet Mohammad was allowed to go beyond the Seventh Heaven, which was the last frontier between God and man. Prophet Mohammad was made to visualize the Kingdom of God beyond Sidratul' Muntaha where no angel or human has ever passed before. Here, Prophet Mohammad was able to understand the vision of a universal culture and spirituality that would transform mankind's self-realization of brotherhood and unity. Prophet Mohammad's request of God to reduce the number of daily prayers from fifty to five was granted. Upon completion of the Night Journey, he was taken back to Mecca.

Energy of the Ascent

Albert Einstein's *Theory of Relativity* states that no one can travel with the speed of light. However, Prophet Mohammad travelled the Universe, which in Earth time was a very short duration.

By making reference to Einstein's Special Theory of Relativity, Hafiz Owais-Ur-Rehman Khan gives a scientific explanation regarding the Isra' and Mi'raj. According to Einstein, if a body travels with the velocity of light, then Time Dilation and Relativity of Simultaneity occur. Prophet Mohammad was riding al-Buraq, and the speed (velocity) of al-Buraq was similar or more than the speed (velocity) of light. In other words, Time Dilation and Relativity of Simultaneity occurred during the event of Mi'raj. Therefore, time either seemed to stop or a very short duration of time passed.

Time distance from the Earth to the edge of the visible Universe is about 46.5 billion light-years in any direction...a diameter of 92.94 billion light-years. Light travels 9.46 trillion kilometers in a year. To travel such a huge distance, billions of years are required. How did Prophet Mohammad travel such a huge distance in a very short duration of time?

Khan goes on to say that a consequence of Special Theory of Relativity is Lorentz' Contraction according to which length seems to be contracted (shorter) for an observer (person) moving with the velocity of light. Therefore, it is possible that one could feel a very short distance while in fact it was a very huge distance. The final consequence is equivalence of mass and energy, $E=mc2$, according to which if a body will travel with the speed (velocity) of light, then its mass will be converted into energy. When this energy will be reconverted into mass, then due to mass defect some amount of mass will disappear. In other words, mass of the body will not join as it was originally.

Even though $E=mc2$ states that there must be variation (mass defect), nothing like that happened to Prophet Mohammad, i.e., no defect was produced. God kept Prophet Mohammad safe from every possible defect. Why this happened cannot be explained via physics, because of the many unknown variables that can have an effect on the consequence. No doubt the Night Journey of Prophet Mohammad was truly a miracle, as he was blessed with the light and energy from God.[84]

In the article, *Prophet Muhammad's Night Journey to the Seven Heavens (peace be upon him)*, the Isra' and Mi'raj defies explanation and seems to defy the laws of physics. A possibility for the occurrence may be that God allowed Prophet Mohammad a shortcut in the three-dimensional (length, width, and height) space by moving him through a higher dimensional space. The journey was not a horizontal or vertical journey in the three dimensions we know of but, rather, through a higher dimension that made travel much faster. Each of the seven heavens might exist yet in even higher dimensions. Therefore, the movement through higher dimensions of space might have made it possible for the whole Night Journey and the events to take place in such a short amount of time, as measured by time in our three-dimensional world. As time is thought to be a fourth dimension, the Night Journey was one beyond the fourth dimension, or beyond time, because everything that happened took place incredibly fast compared to the ordinary flow of time here on Earth. Perhaps, the seven heavens are seven additional dimensions to length, width, height, and time.[85]

The closer one travels at the speed of light, the heavier his mass becomes thereby needing more energy to go faster and, therefore, the amount of energy needed to go further becomes infinite. In other words, the mass itself will need to undergo a change of state to generate the energy required for travelling faster. Light does, however, have a finite speed. During the Isra' and Mi'raj, Prophet Mohammad was supercharged with the light of energy with the transformer generated at full potency, especially since his vehicle was al-Buraq. During the Night Journey of Prophet Mohammad, the rules of physics stopped, as al-Buraq travelled through the Heavens faster than the normal speed of light. This was made possible only by God, as He made exceptions for the Prophets to complete their mission, e.g., Prophet Mohammad's Night Journey or splitting of the Red Sea for Prophet Moses and his followers to cross. God has the power to alter the laws of the speed of light and time that differ from our concept of the normal speed of light and time:

"The angels and the Spirit ascend unto Him in a Day the measure whereof is (as) fifty thousand years." (70:4; Qur'an)

The "Day" in this verse is understood to be a long period of time, for example, an eon. However, the length of time and what happens during that time are not precisely defined.

Like Isra' and Mi'raj, the Night of Power (Laylat-ul-Qadr) took place at night, and each emphasized the importance and practice of prayer. In his article, *Various Dimensions of Miraj*, Imran N. Hosein refers to the verse in the Qur'an, *"The Night of Power is better than a thousand months."* (97:3; Qur'an) Hosein says the implication is that which can best be experienced on that night (namely Mi'raj) in that it is better than an entire lifetime (a thousand months standing for an average life-span) lived without that experience (Mi'raj).[86]

The Night of Power occurs during the month of Ramadan, and it is the holiest night of the year. It is the time when the Qur'an was revealed to Prophet Mohammad. Angels descend on Earth bringing with them God's Blessings, as well as peace for those who seek them through prayers and supplications. As Muslims gather to pray during the Night of Power, they perform many prayers that take a great deal of concentration and energy. A time for fervent and devoted prayers, Muslims feel happiness and joy and a renewed energy with faith and determination.

Imamat

Muslims believe that the concept of Divine Unity is based on the Qur'an and recognition of the Unity of God in all His Attributes, in particular that God alone must be worshipped. Based on their belief in the Divine Unity, the Shi'as maintain that while God is Just in the obligations He imposes on His worshippers, He does not impose obligations on mankind beyond their capabilities. That man is essentially free to choose between right and wrong. His choice to be good or bad is of his own free will, as he will bear the reward or consequence of that choice. The Twelve Imams expounded upon the concept of the free will and volition. The Twelve Imams that succeeded Prophet Mohammad were men of purity, excellence and were equally sinless and infallible. The Twelve Imams are manifested in the Divine Light of guidance, as this Light passed from one Imam to the next. For Shi'as, the Twelve Imams are unified strands within the *Rope of God*.

Picture the *Rope of God* as having two ends. At one end is the Qur'an and at the other end is *Ahl al-Bayt*, the Members of the Family of Prophet Mohammad. Just as the Prophets were a continuation of the previous Prophet, the Members of the Family of Prophet Mohammad are a continuation of the root of Prophet Mohammad. They are called the Twelve Imams. They were infallible and immune to sin; however, they were not Prophets. Prophet Mohammad was the seal of the Prophets. Nonetheless, these Imams possessed similar qualities to those of Prophets. The first Imam is Imam Ali Ibn Abi Talib, the first cousin and son-in-law to Prophet Mohammad. The last Imam is Imam Mohammad al-Mahdi who is still alive in his occultation.

Since man is not self-sufficient to guide himself in terms of faith and religious doctrines, the necessity for Imams arises. While patients may be able to read a book on medicine, they still need a physician to help diagnose and administer a cure for their ailment. Similarly, Imams are needed to continue the work of the Prophet in explaining what the many verses in the Qur'an mean. Centuries have followed since the passing of Prophet Mohammad, and the world has had a dramatic change owing in large part to technology and space travel as well as easy access around the globe. The major role of Imams is to guide the people from ignorance, tyranny and disputes, to mention just a few. After the death of Prophet Mohammad, the Imam was entrusted with the guardianship of the Prophet's accomplishments and the continuation of the Prophet's leadership. In short, the Imam's role was to guide mankind in all aspects of their existence.

The Twelfth Imam is in his occultation, and he will return with Prophet Jesus back to Earth, at which time they both will be in unison with each other as they address the ills of the societies around the world. In the interim, another channel of religious teaching and training is needed. These are the *ulema*, or religious teachers, who are not infallible but are schooled in the philosophy and jurisprudence of Islam making them qualified to impart knowledge on their constituents.

The Prophets and Imams provided guidance and understanding of Islam to their constituents, and these are illustrated quite vividly in many verses in the Qur'an. Following is a discussion of one of the Twelve Imams, Imam Ali Ibn Abi Talib:

Heroic Achievements of Imam Ali Ibn Abi Talib

During his speech at Ghadeer-e-Khum, Prophet Mohammad said:

"Oh people! I performed my Prophetic mission and did put in endeavor to the maximum of my energy that I possess. You should know that I leave two valuable (weighty) things among you after myself (after my death) so that these two will never at all get separated from each other: (1) the Holy Qur'an, the Book of God; and (2) My Ahl al-Bayt (People of the House: Imam Ali; Fatima; Hassan; Hussein; and nine Imams from the descendants of Hussein. I am the guardian (wali) of whosoever, (he should know that) Ali is also his guardian, Oh God! Be the friend of the friends of Ali and be the enemy of his enemies. Help those who help him and be the enemy of anyone who fights him. Yes, those who are present convey my words to those who are not present here. I hope they will lend ears and accept it." [87]

There are numerous heroic achievements of Imam Ali Ibn Abi Talib. Prophet Mohammad needed a great deal of protection to propagate the faith of Islam. Imam Ali was the vehicle of that protection. With respect to courage, bravery, fortitude, and valor, Imam Ali was the essence and perfect example of these virtues:

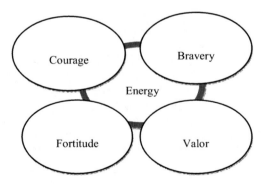

Virtues of Courage, Bravery, Fortitude, and Valor

The self-fulfillment of courage, bravery, fortitude, and valor is best exemplified by Imam Ali who possessed these virtues. We will explore how these virtues manifested in the excellence of Imam Ali's personality, attitude, behavior, and dedication to Islam.

Courage emanated from Imam Ali's conscience, motivations, and thoughts that resulted in protecting Prophet Mohammad, overcoming obstacles, and engaging in heroic feats on the battlefield. Courage was heightened in times of struggles, e.g., war and peace, as Imam Ali acted upon the heroic spirit of conviction inspired by justice and guided by wisdom.

How courage surfaced was by Imam Ali's intention. It was his action evident by a vigilant presence of mind, circumstances known to be difficult and dangerous, and ethically praiseworthy of his righteous intention. His courage was a self-affirmation that enabled him to look past the immediate situation to find the strength to self-regulate, i.e., the self that surpasses itself. His courage was power of the mind to overcome fear. Here, courage was not the absence of fear but, rather, the capability to act in spite of it. As he feared God, he feared nothing else. For Imam Ali, courage was prudent and controlled by a sense of truth and justice that was free of bias and hatred. It was a courage that was humble and non-boastful. His constancy of mind was unshaken, as he faced and endured danger. Truly, he had a sense of honor, duty, and piety.

Imam Ali was driven by an internal courage-fueled energy field that magnified his spirit's fulfillment. Courage sparked his energy and ignited his leadership. Not only did he have the courage to win on the battlefield but also the courage to win the peace. Rather than wage war against those who denied him of his rightful claim to the Caliphate, Imam Ali chose the path of safeguarding Islam against its enemies. For this reason, Imam Ali chose peaceful means by supporting the other Caliphs. So he kept quiet and became patient, even though his right was violated. During that time, the enemies of Islam were awaiting an opportunity to destroy Islam. However, Imam Ali did not give them that opportunity, because he chose the bigger picture, which was to avoid warfare within the Islamic community.

For many, bravery is impulsive, hurried, stubborn, reckless, blind, and furious. But for Imam Ali bravery is fearless, steadfast, and resolute. His bravery was the quality of spirit that enabled him to face danger of pain without showing fear. He did not restrain his fear but, rather, experienced it. In this respect, he held tenaciously to the good, moderating the fear of which he is fully aware. Bravery is physical, while courage is mental and moral. His courage transcended the noble concept of bravery. One can be brave without courage and courageous without bravery, but for Imam Ali he possessed both virtues. The basis of his courage was his love of God. While his bravery was that of a heroic warrior, his courage was steadfast. This was not a case of Imam Ali's bravery in the field of battle but, rather, his bravery in the field of patience.

Without question, Imam Ali, more than anyone else, endured all sorts of hardships for the cause of Islam.

Fortitude is a virtue that restrains one's fear and bravery within reason. It strengthens one's mind against the greatest danger, which is that of death. It is this firmness of mind that enables a person to encounter danger with self-confidence. It is a determination to confront danger or to endure difficulty. For Imam Ali, fortitude fastened his will with impregnable reason, as he confronted his enemies on the battlefield. His steadfastness and resolve removed any obstacles, e.g., fear, as he met danger. He was willing to sacrifice his life for the cause of Islam. He loved what was larger and more important than him, namely, truth, justice, and the common good. His love for God was priority, and he exposed himself to the danger of death protecting Prophet Mohammad and Islam.

Valor is believed to have all the best qualities of both courage and bravery. It exalts in risking all for a just cause. It looks far ahead and is wise. Men are valiant, as they are moved by the higher aims and passions of nature. No man can be valiant for a trifle or a repulsive end. For Imam Ali, what motivated his valor was the love of God, truth, justice, and that which is dignified and noble.

The perfection of Imam Ali's virtues was displayed when he slept in the bed of Prophet Mohammad, in order to protect the Prophet from the enemies who wished to kill him. This act of courage, bravery, fortitude, and valor exhibited his readiness to sacrifice himself for the cause of Islam. Imam Ali slept in Prophet Mohammad's bed to impersonate him and prevent an assassination plot on the life of the Prophet. For Imam Ali to be willing to sacrifice his life, while under the swords ready to strike, represents the highest sense of piety and loyalty. This heroic act allowed the Prophet to safely make his migration to Medina.

During the Battle of the Trench, Imam Ali displayed his power and energy, as he defeated Amru Ibn Abd Wid, the champion of the enemy. Amru Ibn Abd Wid, a ferocious, gallant, and famous warrior, not only challenged but mocked the Muslims as well. Imam Ali accepted the challenge and defeated Amru Ibn Abd Wid. As Imam Ali stood to thrust the sword into Amru, the latter spat in Imam Ali's face. Imam Ali was extremely angered by this act of insult. It took a great deal of self-control for Imam Ali to restrain his anger, so he momentarily postponed killing Amru, until his anger was restrained. Why he waited to kill him was because he didn't want his anger, or negative energy, to be the reason but, rather, his faith. In other words, Imam Ali wanted to be directed and guided by his positive energy. All present at the Battle of the Trench were in awe, as Imam Ali displayed his restraint of anger.

There is a significant difference between the person who is in control of his anger before finishing off his victim and one who is not in control of his anger as he punishes his victim without reflection. Anger simply exists as energy. What one chooses to do with anger determines if it is bad or good. The energy of anger can motivate one into creating a better situation, which is the highest purpose for this energy and why we were given the emotion of anger. Imam Ali was a man in control of his emotions, and his electromagnetic energy waves sparked his temperament toward restraint in time of anger. When Imam Ali recognized and acknowledged his anger, it became positive energy that enabled him to change the situation he was angry about. The heroism of Imam Ali was the most decisive factor in the victory. The defeat of Amru Ibn Abd Wid struck terror in the hearts of the enemy so much that they abandoned the battlefield. This defeat was so devastating for the enemy that the disbelievers gave up their objective to advance to Medina.

Powers of Imam Ali Ibn Abi Talib

In the long history of mankind, there comes a time when someone appears that personifies the ultimate perfection of all that is good and righteous. Such a person stands out as a radiant figure whose presence illuminates the mind, heart, and soul of all who aspire towards perfection in their lives. Such a man was Imam Ali Ibn Abi Talib whose divinely-inspired consciousness was manifested in his personality. He was the reflection of the light of Prophet Mohammad's inner reality and divine reservoir of wisdom.

In his book, *Polarization around the Character of 'Ali Ibn Abi Talib*, Ayatollah Murtada Mutahhari, the renowned scholar and martyr, discusses how the creative energy of Imam Ali is demonstrated in the two-powered personality of polar opposites: attraction and repulsion. Mutahhari expounds on a concept called *elixir*, which is a miraculous substance that transforms one material into another, for example, base metals into gold.[88]

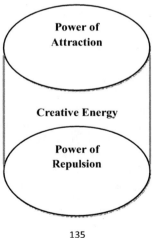

For Imam Ali, true *elixir* is love, and this love is manifested in his power of attraction. Throughout the centuries following his martyrdom, we find many people whose hearts are filled with love and admiration for Imam Ali. As time passes on, this love for Imam Ali becomes more profound and intensified. He was the personification of perfection that transcended beyond his moral virtues of wisdom, eloquence, bravery, and many other characteristics of his divinely-inspired soul. Even the corrupt that he punished, according to the laws of Islam, did not turn away from him for they knew his act was just. People are attracted to Imam Ali, because they can feel in their hearts the very soul of his love that emanates from his inseparable unity with truth. Truly, his power of attraction is eternal.

On the other hand, Imam Ali also had the power of repulsion. There were those who despised him, as he exposed their hypocrisy, deception, ignorance, and deviations. This infuriated his sworn enemies, as they plotted to form false alliances with others against him, ultimately leading to his martyrdom and to the martyrdom of his progeny. By upholding the very sanctity of Islam, Imam Ali had to undertake steps to uproot the ills in the society. As a result, his enemies were pained by his truthfulness and justice.

Imam Ali's creative energy was characterized by his thoughts, feelings, and emotions that personified the true and ideal essence of Islamic morality. It was an energy that resigned itself in humbleness, as he addresses his Lord. His creative energy was relegated toward pleasing God in worship, prayers, and obedience. Teaching, informing, and helping others learn about Islam comprised a great deal of his time and energy. While he stood in the face of deception, betrayal, trickery, hypocrisy, greed, treachery, and chicanery, he was steadfast in upholding the ideals of Islam. It was justice, truth, and freedom of choice that were the engines of his creative energy. Imam Ali was pious and God-fearing. For example, as a warrior, while he was brave and courageous, he was also kind, understanding, compassionate, responsive, and affectionate. He devoted a great deal of his energy tending to the needs of the poor, and his heart was absorbed by his continuous affection and empathy for the afflicted and disadvantaged.

Good and bad are two opposite poles and in any given society there are people that possess both traits: attraction towards the good as well as repulsion from the bad. Imam Ali had both the power of attraction and the power of repulsion. He had very loyal friends as well as wicked enemies that knowingly oppose what is right. We can learn from the experiences of Imam Ali that our human nature is very complex and reflects the complexity of the world around us and the mind that perceives it. Through our senses, we can experience the external environment and categorize our experiences in terms of polarities – positive and negative, attraction and repulsion, pleasure and pain, calm and agitation, love and hate. Like Imam Ali, as we pursue peace, justice, and happiness, it is our human nature to impulsively desire experiences that our body and mind can translate as positive and feel aversion to all that is disturbing and negative.

SYMBOLISM OF THE TRAGEDY AT KARBALA

CHAPTER 10

ENERGY CASE EXAMPLES: HEROES OF ISLAM

God has bestowed upon the most pious individuals the rank of Imam. Relative to mankind, God instilled within each of these Imams the power of intellectuality and leadership, as well as the guardian of all matters relative to religion, the laws that govern the society, and the dynamics and dimensions of mankind's existence. Prophet Abraham had attained the level of Imam:

> "And remember when his Lord tried Abraham with certain Commands, which he fulfilled. He (God) said: 'Verily I make thee an Imam for mankind.' He (Abraham) said: 'And of my offspring?' He (God) answered: 'My covenant is not within the reach of the unjust.'" (Qur'an 2:124)

What this verse means is that Prophet Abraham had completed all the tasks and trials that God had given him. In other words, Prophet Abraham passed all the tests, for example, as God's Servant, as God's Prophet, as the Ideal Character favored by God, and as God's Imam. In addition, only the pious of Prophet Abraham's progeny may reach the level of Imam.

Beginning with Prophet Abraham, the electromagnetic and spiritual energy transferred from one Imam to the next Imam. Like Prophet Abraham, Prophet Mohammad was also an Imam who passed all the tests that God had given him. Likewise, Prophet Mohammad's cousin and son-in-law, Imam Ali, was an Imam as well as his offspring and their progeny who possessed the Divine Attributes given by God.

In a sermon, Imam Ja'far as-Sadiq said the following:

> "God has illumined...the Imams from the Household of the Prophet (Mohammad) and made them the abundant spring from which knowledge of religion gushes forth. Whoever recognizes the claims of the Imams, based on sound knowledge and insight will taste the sweetness of faith and come to know the luminous and beautiful visage of Islam. For God has appointed the Imams to be His Proof among men and their guide; has placed on their heads the crown of sublimity and leadership; caused the light of His own splendor to shine on their beings; and sustained and supported them with inexhaustible Heavenly power...Imam is versed in all the complexities, problems and metaphoric aspects of revelation, and he is chosen by God from among the descendants of Hussein...God has chosen all of them to lead the Ummah (community) in order that they should guide the people and judge justly among them."[89]

This sermon underscores the connectivity between the Imamat and Divine Energy. For example, Imam Hussein possessed the Divine Energy within his character that enabled him to make the ultimate sacrifice of his life for the cause of Islam.

Tragedy of Karbala

Throughout the centuries, the tragedy of Karbala has been revisited and retold over and over again. Including Imam Hussein, there were 138 faithful and courageous Muslims who were martyred in their fight against tyranny and oppression. Their memories have not been forgotten, as this annual remembrance and reenactment of the tragedy has become a tradition. No doubt that Imam Hussein was the catalyst to save Islam. However, without the help of his sister, Lady Zainab, and his son, Imam Ali Zein al-Abideen, the tragedy would have long been forgotten. The following diagram illustrates the role of each of these three heroes of Islam:

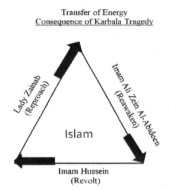

Transfer of Energy
Consequence of Karbala Tragedy

The triad of Imam Hussein, Lady Zainab, and Imam Ali Zein al-Abideen is the continuation of the root of Prophet Mohammad and Imam Ali Ibn Abi Talib. Divine Energy nurtured their bodies, minds, hearts, and souls. God had kept away all impurities by purifying them thoroughly. It was the light of this energy, which transmitted from generation to generation to the Members of the Household of Prophet Mohammad (*Ahl al-Bayt*), that guided their every move and action.

Bear in mind that at the time of the Karbala tragedy there were no televisions, radios, or mass media to broadcast this tragic event. Aside from camels and ships, which would have taken a great deal of time to reach other communities and nations, there was virtually no other medium to inform others of what had transpired at Karbala. There were also no automobiles, airplanes, trains, or other means of transport to get to other areas, including the country of Iraq, of which

Karbala is a city. For all intents and purposes, the tragedy would have been localized to the areas of Karbala and Kufa. Ibn Ziyad, who was loyal to Yazid Ibn Muawiyah, was the governor of Kufa, and he would most assuredly have killed the memory of the tragedy. Let us examine how each of these three heroes reinforced each other:

Imam Hussein

Synopsis of Events that Led to the Karbala Tragedy

Imam Hussein was born in Medina on the 3rd of Shaban in the year 4 A.H. (625 AD) His father was Imam Ali and his mother was Fatima, the daughter of Prophet Mohammad. Regarding Imam Hussein, it is quoted from Prophet Mohammad saying, *"Hussein is from me and I am from Hussein. Whoever loves him, love me. And whoever is his enemy, is my enemy."* Imam Hussein was one of the five included in the following Qur'anic verse:

"...And God only wishes to remove all abomination from you, Members of the Family, and to make you pure and spotless." (Qur'an 33:33)

This verse included Prophet Mohammad, Imam Ali Ibn Abi Talib, Fatima, Imam Hassan, and Imam Hussein. The importance of this revelation must not be underestimated. When the time came for Imam Hussein to stand up for the principles of freedom and justice, he gave his life in defense of Islam.

Yazid was the son of Muawiyah and the grandson of Abu Sufyan, the latter who accepted Islam after finding himself helpless when Prophet Mohammad had control over Mecca. Like his father, Muawiyah, Yazid usurped the title of Caliph. Muawiyah had Imam Hassan, the brother of Imam Hussein, poisoned. Muawiyah then appointed his son, Yazid, to be Caliph after him. Yazid was the embodiment of corruption, wickedness, and cruelty.

Like his father who unjustly ruled for 20 years, Yazid dealt ruthlessly with anyone who dared to say anything against him. He was also self-centered, narcissistic, and egotistical and gave preferential treatment to those opportunistic and worthless people who flattered him, installing them as governors and leaders in the mosques. He denigrated and demeaned the very sanctity of Islam by openly ridiculing Prophet Mohammad and the Members of his Household with derisive and scornful remarks. Human rights were denied. Islam was on the verge of destruction, owing to Yazid's chicanery, insidiousness, and treachery.

There was no alternative but for Imam Hussein to stand up against Yazid who tried to force Imam Hussein to capitulate and surrender to him. However, Imam Hussein would never give allegiance to Yazid, nor would Imam Hussein humiliate and disgrace himself to such a despot. Instead, Imam Hussein remained resolute, as he stood firm against Yazid's demand.

Yazid ordered the Governor of Medina to force Imam Hussein to give his oath of allegiance or have his head cut off. Imam Hussein met with the Governor of Medina, refused his request, and returned to Mecca. Around this time, the people of Kufa, Iraq pledged their allegiance and support for Imam Hussein by sending letters extending an invitation to him. The people of Kufa feared that Islam would be destroyed by the Yazid's greed for power and glory. Imam Hussein sent his cousin, Muslim Ibn Aqeel (nephew of Imam Ali Ibn Abi Talib) to Kufa to assess the seriousness of support from the people of Kufa. While Muslim reported back to Imam Hussein that their support was genuine, he later found out that he was tricked. As Muslim tried in vain to notify Imam Hussein of the trickery, he was not allowed to leave Kufa and was subsequently martyred. At the same time, Yazid had ordered the assassination of Imam Hussein in Mecca. In order to avoid bloodshed on the sacred ground of Mecca, Imam Hussein, along with his family and faithful companions, left Mecca and proceeded to Kufa, unaware of the deception that awaited him. Another turn of events occurred. The people of Kufa, who had pledged their support for Imam Hussein, reneged. Yazid had bribed and threatened the people of Kufa with death, if they supported Imam Hussein. Consequently, Imam Hussein was abandoned and forsaken.

Imam Hussein was besieged by Yazid's army, and he was prevented from continuing to Kufa or from returning home. So Imam Hussein and his party were forced to travel in the desert. Imam Hussein reached Karbala, which is also in Iraq. All his companions, men, women, and children were denied water for two or three whole days, in the blazing heat of the sun and scorching hot sands of Karbala.

On the 10th of the lunar month of Muharram (Ashura) the war began, as the army of the enemies, estimated at over 30,000 soldiers, outnumbered Imam Hussein's small contingent of less than 100 loyal Muslims. That day, Imam Hussein and his followers courageously fought from morning until their final breath, as all the companions and relatives were martyred (except for Imam Ali Zein al-Abideen who was very ill and laid in his tent), which totaled 138 faithful Muslims.[90] Imam Hussein was bombarded with arrows from the enemy. The enemies were heartless and merciless, as they decapitated Imam Hussein and his followers. They spilled the blood of Prophet Mohammad's Household, the blood that stood up for justice and truth. Not only was Imam Hussein maliciously decapitated by the enemy, he was also crushed by the hooves of the horses. Even Wahab Kalbi and his wife gave their lives at Karbala in spite of being Christians. Many Muslims are still unable to understand the inner meaning of Karbala, while there are non-Muslims, such as Wahab Kalbi and his wife, who not only understood it but gave their lives in order to protect Imam Hussein's just cause.

At the conclusion of the battle, the army of the enemy then burned the tents and plundered the helpless women and children. The fallen victims of genocide were denied burial. Under the scorching sun and blistering sands, the women and children walked with chains around their necks and hands. In celebration, the army of Yazid placed the heads of Imam

Hussein and his faithful followers on spears, as they paraded them through the towns and villages. This display was to show that the army of Yazid was prepared to annihilate anyone who would defy Yazid. The bodies of the martyrs were under the scorching sun for three days until a tribe passing that place found them and performed the burial. The head of Imam Hussein was taken to Damascus and presented at the feet of Yazid. How deplorable and vicious was this vile act.

No one has stood up for freedom and justice like Imam Hussein, who sacrificed his life and the lives of his family and faithful Muslims for the sake of Islam. Imam Hussein is truly a great sacrifice in the history of humanity. Each year, the commemoration of Ashura on the 10th of Muharram is reminder of the great sacrifices of Imam Hussein, his family, and the faithful Muslims and what they stood for.

Let us reflect on the martyrdom of Imam Hussein and learn from his example. Remember that Islam cannot be compromised. To know whether or not you have compromised Islam requires that you have knowledge of at least the basic fundamentals of Islam. This requires an understanding of what Islam is and what it is not. When you submit your will to God, are certain of your faith, believe in Imam Hussein's message, and accept the challenge that you will strive in the way of God to better yourself as a Muslim. Be steadfast and actionable in your obligation to Islam. Display the right attitude so that your faith can endure. Let your behavior be one for others to follow, and above all be patient!

Revolt

Revolution for Imam Hussein was not to enhance his stature in the Islamic world but, rather, to establish justice and release the community from oppression and tyranny. In essence, Imam Hussein wanted to restore the people back to the right path of Islam. Imam Hussein's objective was not for glory or for power but, rather, for the supreme sacrifice to save Islam. Imam Hussein wanted to restore to the people their dignity and self-respect and to instill the true meaning of brotherhood. Imam Hussein did not revolt until all options had been exhausted. When he came to the realization that the only way to transform the community back to the Islam his grandfather, Prophet Mohammad, had preached was to sacrifice his own life toward that cause. In essence, Imam Hussein's revolt was a struggle (*jihad*) only in defense of Islam, as he had to rise against the tyrannical Umayyad regime of Yazid Ibn Muawiyah.

Imam Hussein revolted to restore Islamic law. He stepped up to the challenge, and with his bravery and courageous spirit he was victorious. For in this victory, he reawakened the consciousness of the people. Following in the footsteps of his father, Imam Ali, he took upon himself the social responsibility of the community (*Ummah*), for that community was the community of his father and grandfather. As such, he fulfilled his responsibility and obligation with determination and sincerity, as he sacrificed his life and that of the members of his family and his friends, so that he could restore freedom, truth, and justice as well as Qur'anic law to the community (*Ummah*).

The most important factor for which Imam Hussein undertook his revolt was to clean up the Islamic caliphate from the Umayyad corruption that they had usurped unjustly, because the caliphate of that time was not a medium of establishment of injustice and removal of backwardness and mischief from the world in a way Islam desired. Islam considers the institution of caliphate as an important agency for spreading truth and justice among the people. Therefore, if the caliphate is righteous, the entire nation shall also be righteous. If the caliphate deviated from its responsibility, the community shall fall into terrible turmoil and calamities. On the basis of this, Imam Hussein rose up so that he may restore to the Islamic Caliphate an illuminated existence and brilliant future.

The martyrdom of Imam Hussein was the changing point in the history of Muslims and their life. Suddenly there was a complete change in them, and they became armed with determination and resolve and all those obstacles that had restrained them were removed and they were released. The clouds of fear and submissions that had imprisoned them changed into a revolution and confrontation.[91]

Spiritual Energy

Yazid and his immoral followers polluted their human energy fields. As such, their energy fields were blocked, and the only outcome was depraved and evil acts. Committing vile acts repeatedly made their energy system inert and lifeless.

In analyzing the characteristics of Imam Hussein, more than any other of his divine qualities, it is the bravery and the greatness of his soul that attracts the attention. Immersed in this energy, Imam Hussein's objective in life and his holy uprising against injustice was far from satisfying his personal needs and interests. His noble soul was and remains unique throughout history. His humbleness, valor, magnanimity, faith, sincerity, and love for justice, are certainly unmatched. With such impeccable personal qualities, he cannot be considered as an ordinary person.

Imam Hussein shouldered the tasks of the Prophets of the past, and for this reason he is rightly considered as an heir and legatee to such divine Prophets as Adam, Noah, Abraham, Moses, Jesus, and Mohammad. Imam Hussein is a symbol of bravery, patience, and resistance in the face of the worst systems of injustice. Prophet Mohammad's grandson triumphed in martyrdom, and continued to teach to generations the values of freedom and justice and the need to confront oppression and tyranny.[92]

According to the First Law of Thermodynamics, energy cannot be created or destroyed. So where does the energy of Imam Hussein come from? He was endowed with certain genetic characteristics and his will that have the potential to manifest super abilities. However, we know from science that these genes by themselves do not generate super abilities. Imam Hussein had a great source of positive energy, which was transmitted to him genetically from his parents, Imam Ali and Fatima. He was able to pull energy from the spiritual world into the physical world through the transmission of energy from his parents and the lineage before them. This is the energy that Imam Hussein used to manifest his abilities. This source of energy from the spiritual world was nurtured and transmitted to Imam Hussein by the Grace of God.

The energy that Imam Hussein emits in the form of radiation has to come from somewhere. He draws energy from the spiritual world, which he emits as radiation. In other words, when Imam Hussein speaks or counsels or conducts his daily affairs, he radiates and illuminates those in his presence. In other words, people who come in contact with Imam Hussein are in awe by his presence, which is one of purity and righteousness. With Imam Hussein, he had the perfect balance physically, emotionally, mentally, and spiritually. For Imam Hussein, this balance resulted in the perfect self, i.e., he vibrated at a higher level so he had unmistakable clarity. The electromagnetic energy that emanated from Imam Hussein's thoughts and actions transformed the community (*Ummah*). The electrical wavelengths and magnetic currents of Imam Hussein, when super-energized, enlightened the Muslims to regain the Islam of his grandfather, Prophet Mohammad.

Lady Zainab

Characteristics

Perhaps no female in the history of mankind personified the essence of patience (*sabr*) more than Lady Zainab. Through all the adversities she and her family suffered, she remained steadfast and patient in her worship of God. This patience was an act of worship – the highest level of worship – as she exhibited her resolve, even though she had been mentally abused and harassed as a captive of the evil, malicious, and illegitimate ruler, Yazid. Offering her two young sons to be martyred with her brother, Imam Hussein, and five other brothers on the field of Karbala was an act of worship.

We must ask ourselves as to what would have happened if Lady Zainab were not in Karbala at the time of the tragedy. Most assuredly, 'Ubaydullah Ibn Ziyad, Governor of Kufa, would have silenced the tragedy and have propagated the incident to the benefit of the ruthless Umayyad regime. As a result, the martyrdom of Imam Hussein and his faithful followers would have withered away in the desert sands of Karbala. Had it not been for Lady Zainab, the tragedy of Karbala would have faded into oblivion. Women were not expected to engage in *jihad* (struggle) in defense of Islam, but Lady Zainab stepped up to the challenge and most willingly offered herself in the defense of Islam and the *Ahl al-Bayt* (Members of the Household of Prophet Mohammad).

With courage and determination, Lady Zainab hurried to the battlefield of Karbala. She stood over the mortal remains of her brother, Imam Hussein. The enemies watched and observed her patience, as she stood in the face of the dreadful sight of her brother's martyrdom. With serenity and the passion of her faith and belief, she steadfastly looked to the heavens and said, *"O God, please accept this sacrifice from us."* Rather than Lady Zainab as the captive, the enemies themselves were captivated and mesmerized by the radiance of her persona and the eloquence of her speech. This display of electromagnetic energy that emanated from deep within her soul was the first spark of revolution against Yazid and his Umayyad regime. Following is a snapshot of the virtues of Lady Zainab that she acquired from the Members of the Household of Prophet Mohammad, and which together formed a powerful energy force:

Virtues as a Source of Energy
<u>Characteristics of Lady Zainab</u>

- Sincere – Trustworthy – Loyal – Self-Denial – Supportive – Self-Discipline

- Pious – Judicious – Eloquent – Pure – Righteous – Humble

- Self-Control – Patient – Tolerant – Courageous – Admirable – Heroic

Reproach

It was the eloquence of her speech and the aura of holiness that enveloped Lady Zainab, as she reproached the enemies of Islam, particularly Ibn Ziyad and Yazid. Through reproach, she confronted her enemies by admonishing and rebuking them for their evil crimes against humanity.

In his book, *Lady Zaynab (Peace Be Upon Her)*, Badr Shahin gives a thorough accounting of what had transpired during Lady Zainab's captivity.[93] The following will summarize the events of captivity, as documented by Badr Shahin:

Bound with ropes and forced to ride on saddleless, lean camels, the ladies and orphans of Prophet Mohammad's family were taken as captives to Kufa. Her first address of reproach was to the crowds surrounding her caravan, as she and her companions were disgracefully paraded through the streets of Kufa. The people of Kufa had earlier reneged on their support for Imam Hussein and deserted him.

Lady Zainab's eloquent speech rebuked the people of Kufa so effectively, exposed their false faith in Islam, falsified their deceitful tears, and introduced them as the most ignoble criminals, as they contributed strongly in the murder of killing Imam Hussein, his household, and his companions. With the utterance of justice and honesty and the voice of courage and right, Lady Zainab admonished the people of Kufa and pointed to their lowliness and rottenheartedness. Their forgery and falsehood could not deceive her, as she reproached them for their crimes and ascribed to them the meanest characters. Moreover, she commented on their weeping by saying that they should have wept for the big crime of disappointing Imam Hussein and letting him down.

'Ubaydullah Ibn Ziyad, son of the notorious Marjanah, was Governor of Kufa. He was whacking the holy head of Imam Hussein with his baton. He then confronted Lady Zainab with disdain and contempt by saying, *"Thanks to God Who unmasked, killed, and belied your revolution."* Lady Zainab replied:

"Thanks God Who honored us with his Prophet and purified us from uncleanness thoroughly. It is only the lewd whom is unmasked, and it is only the dissolute that is belied. We are not any of these two. Indeed, we are not any of these two, son of Marjanah!"

Her rebuttal to Ibn Ziyad exposed and disgraced him in a way that was worse than a wound caused by spears. Ibn Ziyad became inflamed and threatened to cut off the head of Lady Zainab's nephew, Imam Ali Zein al-Abideen, the son of Imam Hussein. However, Lady Zainab stood firm and said, *"If you want to kill him, kill me with him as well."* Thanks to Lady Zainab, Imam Ali Zein al-Abideen was saved from the tyrant.

From Kufa, Lady Zainab and her family and followers were taken to Damascus. At the palace, Yazid was beating Imam Hussein's head with a stick. Yazid showed his great rejoicing at the current situation, as the family of Prophet Mohammad was captive and the heads of the Prophet's grandsons were thrown before him. Yazid was overjoyed to have Prophet Mohammad's household killed, as Yazid claimed it was revenge against Prophet Mohammad and Imam Ali Ibn Abi Talib for having humiliated his father (Muawiyah) and grandfather (Abu Sufyan) and killing his forefathers during the battle of Badr some years earlier. Lady Zainab addressed Yazid with one of the most spectacular revolutionary speeches in Islam. Lady Zainab smashed the despotism of Yazid and inflicted disgrace and dishonor on him and on those who caused him to reach such a position.

Briefly, she admonished Yazid by referring to the false elation of Yazid who thought of himself as victorious in that encounter at Karbala. She uncovered the truth that his military superiority was transient and that God let the unbelievers enjoy bliss in this world so that their sons will increase and, thus, they will have a painful chastisement on the Day of Resurrection. She reproached Yazid for taking the harem of Prophet Mohammad's Household as captives. The speech of Lady Zainab was one of the deathblows that snapped the Umayyad State. Having seen the collapse of his pride and arrogance, Yazid could not find any words to answer, except a poetic verse not at all related to the subject.

Charismatic Energy

The energy powers of Lady Zainab are surrounded by a concentration of energy or an energy field that interacted and was immersed with energy fields of Prophet Mohammad's Household. In fact, all of the energy fields of Prophet Mohammad's Household interacted with each other that brought about a very potent force.

Lady Zainab's energy radiation was expressed in different ways. For example, the energy that is produced by thoughts and emotions is the form, which is based on the energy radiation that emanates from Lady Zainab, even from her magnetism or charisma. This produced an energy identity that caused a vibration in the energy field that had the power to win over and influence people. Lady Zainab exhibited positive energy. Ibn Ziyad and Yazid both exhibited negative energy that deformed the flow of their thoughts and emotions, for example, their anger, weakness, confusion, and distress. It was in this light that Lady Zainab was able to capitalize on their negative energy to expose their malevolence and evil schemes.

Lady Zainab, with her charisma and eloquence of speech, was able to influence the thoughts and emotions, for example, of the many people who surrounded her caravan as it was disgracefully paraded through the streets of Kufa. Her words radiated each spectator to the point that they began to weep. In effect, she was able to change their moods from one of jeers to one of remorse, sorrow, and guilt.

Even today, Lady Zainab's energy field is able to attract millions of visitors to her shrines, as they pay their respect to Her Eminence. These visitors are both Shi'a and Sunni Muslims who are united in their respect and admiration for Lady Zainab. In other words, this absorbed energy has influenced, even today, innumerable visitors to her shrines. At these shrines, the first thing that becomes perceptible is a change in atmosphere. This change imposes a silence in the mind, so that we receive the messages that the shrines radiate.

For Lady Zainab, the operation of her mind is a manifestation of energy known as electricity, magnetism, and light, which emanate from the underlying force of vibration. Thought vibrations and waves reproduce and send forth similar vibrations so that others may feel the thoughts. Witness how Hind, the wife of Yazid, was impacted by these vibrations and quickly came to the rescue of Lady Zainab. Even this type of vibration energy enveloped Hurr, as he left the camp of the enemy to join forces with Imam Hussein. No doubt, Imam Hussein's energy field was so strong that it sent vibration waves to the mind of Hurr, who then regained his Islamic self.

It was through the medium of vibrating sound waves that Lady Zainab was able to convince her audience. In other words, Lady Zainab's mind, in the manifestation of thoughts in her brain, generated a form of energy of intensely high vibratory waves to the brains of others within her field of influence. Truly, this was manifested between all phenomena of electrical and magnetic energy on the one hand and the phenomena of mental energy on the other.

Lady Zainab played a major role in spreading the account of the tragedy at Karbala. She also protected and supported Imam Ali Zein al-Abideen. In addition, she was able to convince a whole new generation of Muslims to the way of *Ahl al-Bayt* (Household of Prophet Mohammad). Her powerful and influential sermons in Kufa and Damascus aroused the ignorance of people who were deceived by the tyranny of Ibn Ziyad and Yazid.

Kinetic Energy

Kinetic Energy is the energy of motion. Lady Zainab was a leader that manifested her kinetic energy in a positive and effective manner. She had a compelling vision to restore the great name of *Ahl al-Bayt* (Household of Prophet Mohammad). Her inspiring vision was focused on direction and purpose. A leader, she exhibited her kinetic energy to not only capture the audience with her eloquent communication but also to catch them emotionally. As her transparent life was authentic and had the power of attracting people, she set the example for others to follow. By transparency, Lady Zainab's actions were believable and gained the respect of not only her followers but her enemies as well.

With all the potential energy (stored energy) of knowledge she acquired from her father and grandfather, she adroitly and skillfully put it into motion (kinetic energy) to win over the Muslim and non-Muslim communities. She was not only an eloquent speaker but a teacher as well, as she educated, encouraged, demonstrated, and counseled the Muslim community to be more vigilant and actionable as to their Islamic obligations.

As a kinetic leader, she had definable, measurable standards of performance, and she encouraged the Muslim community to be responsible and accountable in upholding the duties and obligations of Islam. She was discontent with the status quo in which the Muslim community sat idly by allowing Yazid to oppress and terrorize them. Consequently, she took the leadership into her own hands to expose the evil machinations of Yazid and his cohorts. Most importantly, Lady Zainab knew that her stand against the transgressors was not a destination but, rather, a continuous life-long journey for all Muslims to follow. Lady Zainab knew that her reproach was not short term but, rather, one of consistency and discipline to execute her grievances against tyranny.

Lady Zainab inspired trust and knew how to lead. She demonstrated her leadership by being an advocate for the people she represented. She created an environment where her followers took pride in themselves as Muslims, as they displayed positive energy in restoring the *Ummah* (Muslim community) back to the morals, ethics, and ideals of Islam. With a reservoir of ideas (potential energy) inherited from Prophet Mohammad's Household), she confront the transgressors by putting these ideas into motion (kinetic energy). Remarkably, she was able to have the Muslim community overcome their inertia energy (resistance to change) and convert it to kinetic energy. Of course, she possessed divine qualities that enabled her to successfully bring about this change.

Rich Whitney and Livia D'Andrea, in their essay on *The Process of Becoming a Leader: An Individual Identity Model*, shed light on the qualities of becoming a leader. They state that the acceptance or kinetic stage is based on kinetic energy. The leader is forever changed, expanded, and validated by the sense of accomplishment. Moreover, the leader is more comfortable with decisions and has a stronger sense of self and assuredness regarding actions and decisions.[94] There is no doubt that Lady Zainab had these qualities.

Effective leadership is characterized by the ability to facilitate positive changes, and Lady Zainab was a true leader. Her well-developed sense of self enabled her to lead with equality, trust, empathy, and integrity. Self-efficacy refers to what Lady Zainab believes about her own ability and her confidence in performing and achieving her goal. In other words, she believed in her capacity and knew her own leadership potential. Self-efficacy is future oriented and about motivation and the need for self-determination and accepting responsibility. Lady Zainab's self was dynamic and encompassed forward moving energy based on her experience and self-efficacy, which transcended into meeting future challenges. Consequently, she carried out her Islamic responsibility by leading the Muslim community back to Islam.

Imam Ali Zein al-Abideen (Imam as-Sajjad)

Imam Ali Zein al-Abideen was the infallible Fourth Holy Imam. He is the son of Imam Hussein and the nephew of Lady Zainab. Together, the three formed the triad of protecting Islam and bringing the Muslim community back to Islam. Imam Ali Zein al-Abideen was given the title of Syed-us-Sajideen or Imam as-Sajjad because of his continuous prostration in prayers and devotion to God. He was praying to God not for glory but, rather, for anything good that happens as well as for the favor of God. He would pray for long durations, especially during the night, and would pray numerous prayers of gratitude. As he was very ill during the tragedy at Karbala, he was unable to participate as a warrior in the battle.

After the conclusion of the Karbala event, Imam as-Sajjad was held captive with his aunt, Lady Zainab, and their followers of women and children. The humiliation and insults inflicted upon him by Ibn Ziyad and Yazid, both wanting to cut his head off, was far more difficult than had he been martyred on the field of Karbala. His *jihad* (struggle) was of a different nature, i.e. to protect his family and followers as well as to bring the *Ummah* (Muslim community) back to the basics of Islam.

Reawaken

With the help of his aunt, Lady Zainab, Imam as-Sajjad confronted Ibn Ziyad and Yazid and exposed their evil intentions and schemes. He would so eloquently use verses from the Qur'an as his guide in addressing them and the Umayyad regime. Threatened to be put to death because his lectures had a positive huge impact on his listeners, it was Lady Zainab who always came to his rescue by eloquently mesmerizing and captivating the tyrants with her speeches as well as offering herself to be killed with her nephew.

Imam as-Sajjad also mesmerized and captivated the mind of Yazid by the power of reason and questions so much that Yazid ordered the Muazzin (one who summons people to prayer) to give Azan (call to prayer) in order to silence Imam as-Sajjad. When the Muazzin uttered the words, *"Ash hadu anna Mohammadan Rasulullah,"* (I bear witness that Mohammad is God's Messenger), this opened the door for Imam as-Sajjad to stop the Muazzin and pursue the questioning of Yazid as to why he would mock Prophet Mohammad and have the family of Prophet Mohammad killed. Yazid was speechless thereby freeing the enslaved minds of the audience to uncover the crimes of Yazid by blaming him for his atrocities against Prophet Mohammad's Household. Fearing for his own life, Yazid released Imam as-Sajjad, Lady Zainab, and all their followers, as they then proceeded to Medina with full honor and respect.

In Medina, Imam as-Sajjad immediately began to apprise the citizens of the horrid tragedy of Karbala, their unwarranted captivity, and the blasphemy of Ibn Ziyad and Yazid and their Umayyad regime. For the rest of his life, Imam as-Sajjad continued to lecture about the evils of tyranny and oppression. He compiled a list of his Supplications, known as *al-Sahifa al-Sajjadiyyah al-Kamilah (The Psalms of Islam)*. It consists of 68 Duas (Supplications), 14 additional Duas, and 15 Munajaat (Whispered Prayers).[95]

As he reawakened the Muslim community by preaching the true Islam in the vicinity of Medina and Mecca, he inspired many people. The Umayyad regime slowly began to realize the dangers that faced them from Imam as-Sajjad's lectures. Years later, the tyrant ruler, Walid Ibn Abdul Malik, had the Governor of Medina poison Imam as-Sajjad. Another chapter in the martyrdom of Prophet Mohammad's Household came to an end. However, the legacy that Imam as-Sajjad left with his Supplications did not end. His Supplications have inspired the minds of Muslims for centuries to follow, and today many Muslims and non-Muslims are genuinely moved by the mastery and eloquence of his writings.

It was Imam as-Sajjad who continued the cause of Islam which his father had courageously died for. The Muslim world had to be reawakened to Islam, and it was Imam as-Sajjad who successfully restored and recovered the Muslims back to the straight path. How he did this was by his example, and his example was prayer, the root essence of Islam. His numerous prayers and supplications are recorded in volumes of books, and they are the standard for all Muslims to follow. One of the special characteristics of Imam as-Sajjad was his piety and self-restraint. Like his grandfather, Imam Ali Ibn Abi Talib, Imam as-Sajjad had the same qualities and attributes in his personality. He was the complete personification of patience, tolerance, forgiveness, and self-sacrifice.

Manifestation of Energy in Prayer and Supplication

While the prayers and speeches of Imam as-Sajjad exhibited his kinetic energy (energy in motion), at the same time it also exhibited his potential energy (stored energy), because his writings and Supplications were stored and contained in volumes of books for all to read and reflect on. Potential energy can be thought of as energy stored within a physical system, such as a book. It is called potential energy, because it has the potential to be converted into another state of energy, such as kinetic energy and to do work in the process. Once the book is being read, potential energy converts to kinetic energy. *An-noor* (light) inspired Imam as-Sajjad to constantly radiate energy of his *nafs* (self). His self had a high intensity of light frequency that radiated clarity of thoughts and actions in his prayers, supplications, and speeches.

Imam as-Sajjad had all the potential energy within him to teach the Muslim community. However, he had to bring the community back to the basics in Islam, because a great deal of the religious doctrines had not been observed owing to the tyrannical regime of Yazid. Muslims were lost and had gone astray during the turbulent times of oppression. They had tainted the very sanctity of the practical obligations of Islam: prayer, fasting, charity, pilgrimage, and *jihad* (struggle). They needed to be guided and reprogrammed to the Islamic way of life. This was not an easy task. Had it not been for Imam as-Sajjad, Islam most certainly would have been a discarded tenet of the past. Imam as-Sajjad had to spend long hours and sleepless nights in trying to remedy the irresponsive and inattentive behavior of the Muslim community.

Imam as-Sajjad had to inculcate in the minds of the Muslim community the following:

- Prayer is the adoration, praise, and obedience to God.

- Prayer is an invocation of the heart and a conscious effort to connect with God.

- Prayer is a time to express and refresh our spiritual potential.

- Prayer and supplication equips us to handle energy effectively.

- Prayer and meditation release positive energy to express our thoughts.

The intensity and devotion of Imam as-Sajjad's prayers and supplications proved him to be admired and followed by the Muslim community, who had to come to grips with their inner self. They needed to understand how the physical, emotional, mental, and spiritual aspects operate within their human energy fields. Imam as-Sajjad had to instill in their minds and hearts the importance of concentration to replace the negative energy with positive energy. Their stresses, anxieties, depression, lack of will were all issues that blocked their energy fields. Clearing these blockages through activation of a vibrant life force energy flow into their systems would help bring positive changes in their lives.

What Imam as-Sajjad did was to instill in the Muslims the importance of bringing the physical, emotional, mental, and spiritual energies into equilibrium and balance with each other. Toward this end, the optimum flow of energy through the entire human system empowers a person with more energy as well as providing a healthy Islamic life.

At the time of the illegitimate Umayyad regime, the *Ummah* (Muslim community) was victim to the tyranny of Yazid and, as such, were distracted from their obligations to Islam. Their spiritual state was disconnected from the rest of their energy field. Imam as-Sajjad embarked on the road to recovery, i.e. to help reduce these distractions and to return their bodies and minds to a balanced state of equilibrium. Meditation helped reduce these distractions albeit it took time, commitment, and patience to achieve a higher level of consciousness. Reconnecting to their positive energy field helped them find the truth about who they truly were, and at the same time it helped them achieve peace and tranquility. Nonetheless, it took many years for the Muslim community to overcome the tyrannical Umayyad and Abbasid regimes. However, thanks to Imam as-Sajjad, the spark of recovery and resurgence was well underway.

Prophet Mohammad based the Islamic government on Islamic laws and principles. It was necessary for each Imam to fulfill this obligation, and to ensure that these Islamic laws and principles were practiced and upheld. While each Imam struggled to uphold the Islamic system of justice, their lives were always in danger resulting in their martyrdom. Only Imam al-Mahdi, the Twelfth Imam, survived the ages. Imam as-Sajjad lived in very difficult times, as he had to survive the tragic event of Karbala and to bear the imprisonment and mistreatment of Yazid from the moment his Imamat began. Then he had to work secretly to spread the true meaning of Islam, as he did with his supplications and whispered prayers.

The triad of Imam Hussein, Lady Zainab, and Imam as-Sajjad truly protected Islam and upheld the Islamic system of justice. Their sacrifices paved the way for Islam to survive and flourish throughout many nations. These three heroes of Islam, who were the continuation of the root of their forefathers, reinforced each other and kept the hopes and prayers of all who espouse freedom and justice alive. We are indebted to their sacrifices, for today we have the freedom to act and practice our faith of Islam. We can raise our heads high, as our hearts and minds are filled with happiness and gratitude for having such leaders as these three heroes to protect us. The tragedy of Karbala instills in us the energy that transcends time itself. As we commemorate the event each year to embrace the energy of Imam Hussein, Lady Zainab, and Imam as-Sajjad, we heighten our awareness of the sacrifices that we also need to be make in order to protect and sustain Islam. May God shower them with His Blessings.

ENERGY AND SCIENCE

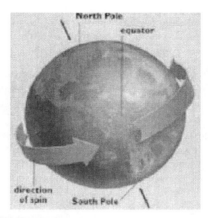

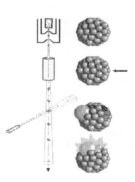

CHAPTER 11

ENERGY AND SCIENCE: CONTRIBUTIONS OF IMAM JA'FAR AS-SADIQ

Imam Ja'far as-Sadiq, the Sixth of the Twelve Infallible Imams, made many contributions to understanding the concept of energy and its relationship to philosophy and science. He was born in the year 702 and martyred in the year 765. Divinely inspired, Imam as-Sadiq exhibited perfection in many areas some of which were medicine, theology, philosophy, mathematics, and science. A thesis conducted by the Research Committee at Strasbourg, France was based on the life of Imam Ja'far as-Sadiq.[96]

The Research Committee included twenty-five world-renown scholars and scientists – mostly non-Muslims – who collaborated together to unanimously confirm the many scientific discoveries made by Imam Ja'far as Sadiq. These scholars are from universities, such as the University of Brussels, University of Paris, University of Strasbourg, University of London, University of Tehran, University of Chicago, University of Lyon, and the University of Freiburg. Among these scholars and scientists was the 1997 Nobel Prize winner in physics, Claude Cohen Tannoudji of the University of Paris, and Francesco Gabrieli, Professor of Arabic Languages and Literatures of the University of Rome. Sayed Musa al-Sadr, the renowned Islamic scholar from Lebanon, was also a member of this Research Committee.[97]

From that Research Committee are excerpts of some of the discoveries made by Imam as-Sadiq some thirteen centuries ago:

- *Discovery of Hydrogen in Water*. His father, Imam Mohammad al-Baqir had discovered the presence of hydrogen in water, which he also found that it was also a highly inflammable gas and that water could be turned into fire. They could not have identified hydrogen without separating it from water through the process of hydrolysis, which is impossible without a strong current of electricity. It was not until the year 1766 when the English scientist, Henry Cavendish, was able to hydrolyze water and obtain hydrogen and to also prove that hydrogen is highly inflammable. What is interesting is that during Imam as-Sadiq's time electricity was not available. Today, the pollution of air rising from excessive use of fossil fuel for producing energy has caused Americans to consider using hydrogen as an alternative source of energy.[98]

- *Theory of Light*. Imam as-Sadiq said that light reflected by different objects comes to us, but only a part of the rays enter our eyes. That is why we do not see distant objects clearly. If all the rays of light that come from them entered our eyes, objects would

155

appear near to us. It was this theory, which helped Lippershey of Flanker's to make his first field glasses or binoculars in 1608. Galileo made use of these binoculars and invented his telescope in 1610. If Imam as-Sadiq had not formulated his theory of light, binoculars and telescopes would not have been invented and made and Galileo could not have confirmed through visual observation the theories of Copernicus and Kepler that all planets including the Earth, rotate around the sun.[99]

- *Matter and Anti-Matter*. One of the theories of Imam as-Sadiq is that everything, except God, has its opposite, but this does not result in a conflict, otherwise the whole Universe would be destroyed. The difference between matter and anti-matter is that in matter the electrons are negatively charged and protons are positively charged. But in anti-matter the electrons are positively charged and protons are negatively charged. Scientists are of the opinion that if one kilogram of matter collides with on kilogram of anti-matter so much energy will be released that the whole world will be destroyed. But no one has so far conducted an experiment to find out what would actually happen if matter collides with anti-matter.[100] Although electrons, protons, and neutrons were not discovered before Imam as-Sadiq arrived, they were still the subject of interest for scientists and philosophers. Even the Qur'an alludes to electrons, protons, and neutrons, and that is what led Imam as-Sadiq to discover them.

- *Light of the Stars*. Imam as-Sadiq said that among the clusters of stars, which we see at night, some are so bright that our sun, in comparison, is quite insignificant. During his time and centuries to follow, many scientists considered his theory to be unacceptable. They could not believe that these small specs of light (stars) could have more light than the light of the sun. About thirteen centuries after the death of Imam as-Sadiq, it was proved that what he had said was correct. It had been discovered that there are stars in the Universe, which are billions of times brighter than the sun. They are called quasars.[101]

- *Theory of Perpetual Motion*. Imam as-Sadiq said that everything in the Universe, including inanimate objects, is always in motion although we may not see it. There is nothing that is without motion. This theory, which was unacceptable in his time, is a scientific fact today. Motion is the essence of being. If there is no motion, there is no existence. He said that it seems to us that when a person dies, his actions and movements come to an end. It is not so. They will continue in another form. Even if the smallest particles of the human body are converted from matter into energy, they will continue to move in the form of energy until the end of time. He added that we feel the passing of time, because of our internal movement. Similarly, our sense of space is due to this movement. Without it, we cannot feel the passage of time and have a sense of space.

There are two kinds of motion in every object - motion inside the atoms and perpetual vibration within the molecules.[102]

- *Theory of Four Elements*. At age 11, Imam as-Sadiq attacked the theory of rotation of the sun around the Earth. At age 12, he rejected the Theory of Four Elements of Aristotle and proved that it was wrong. For a thousand years, Aristotle's Theory of Four Elements remained the cornerstone of physics. No scholar expressed his doubts in accuracy. Imam as-Sadiq said, "I wonder how a man like Aristotle could say that in the world there are only four elements of earth, water, fire, and air. The air is not an element. It contains many elements. Each metal, which is in the earth, is an element." He said that there are many elements in the air and that all of them are essential for breathing. It was not until the 18th century that the father of modern chemistry, Lavoisier, separated oxygen from the air and demonstrated the important role it plays in breathing and combustion that scientists accepted that air is not an element.[103]

- *Rotation of the Earth on its Axis*. Imam as-Sadiq stated that the Earth rotates on its own axis. Most recently, when astronauts landed on the moon, they directed their telescopes towards the Earth and observed that it was, in fact, rotating slowly on its axis. Amazingly, only by knowing the Laws of Mechanics of stars, which was discovered centuries later, did Imam as-Sadiq make this discovery.[104]

Imam Ja'far as-Sadiq recognized the importance of electromagnetic energy on the human system. He had stated:

"There are some lights which, if thrown from a sick person to a healthy person, can possibly make that healthy person sick."[105]

We can conclude from this quote that Imam as-Sadiq was explaining the importance of vibrations in the healing process. Electromagnetic energy generated the vibrations, and the electrical impulses are the *"lights."*

In Islam, placing one's hands on parts of the body of another person, while at the same time reciting prayers or supplications, may result in healing via electrical vibrations. As the hands are on the same frequency as the brain, they can also act as receptors and sensors of electromagnetism. It takes deep meditation by both the healer and the one being healed for the healing process to work. The end result is one of turning negative frequencies into positive frequencies.

Truly, Imam Ja'far as-Sadiq was ahead of his time, and today the recipients of his knowledge and discoveries are beginning to realize the genius of this great person in the history of mankind. His contributions to mankind could only have been accomplished by the Will and

Grace of God. By consensus, the Father of Chemistry is Abu Musa Jabir Ibn Hayyan al Azdi, also known as Geber, was a student of Imam Ja'far as-Sadiq.[106]

EPILOGUE

Energy is everywhere. It surrounds us. We thrive on it. We cannot survive without it. Sometimes we sense it. Sometimes we feel it. Sometimes we hear it. All animals, plants and humans need it to live. Without energy, flowers would not bloom. Without energy, we would not be able to walk, talk, think, or eat. Without energy, we would not be able to pray and fast.

Without energy, the Universe and Earth would cease to function. The same energy directs the Universe and everything in it, every moment of every day. It precisely and predictably determines the form, nature, path and outcome of all things. It directs the life and outcome of every person on Earth.

Everything in the Universe suggests that the natural flow of energy is toward positive abundance – that is, a sufficient and ever increasing supply of conditions that result in improved outcomes. The Universe is expanding, for example, and life is evolving toward greater adaptability and fitness.

Life is a system of energy. Everything is a form of energy. Energy flows in consonance with the flow of life. Our bodies need energy. Our brain needs energy. Our whole human system needs energy. Even the spirit is a form of electrical energy that sustains the life within our bodies, and when we die the spirit, or energy, is released. In accordance with the laws of physics, all forms of energy may be transformed into each other, given the appropriate conditions.

This powerful, all encompassing force, which we call energy, produces every outcome and impacts each of us in far greater ways than most of us have ever imagined. It powers our sun and the many products we regularly enjoy. It powers, directs and defines our lives on every level and in every way. Everything that exists in the Universe is made up of energy. Every atom has energy. We direct energy to a far greater extent than most believe, and the way we manage it has a direct impact on our lives, from a personal level to a global one.

If everything is energy, it stands to reason then that everything, including humans, must obey the laws that govern energy. Humans harness and direct energy in much the same way as it is harnessed and directed for electricity. As humans, our main objective is to attain and sustain a balanced flow of internal energy. This balance enables the physical, mental, emotional, and spiritual levels of our energy fields to be healthier.

For purposes of this book, I discussed the importance of energy as it relates to the Islamic obligations of prayer and fasting. Other obligations, such as charity, pilgrimage and *jihad* (struggle) are also impacted by energy. For example, energy of consciousness is stored

159

(potential energy) until it is moved (kinetic energy) to almsgiving. When air temperature exceeds body temperature, the body gains heat energy that converts into mechanical energy when performing the circumambulation during the pilgrimage. Exerted effort and struggle (*jihad*) elicit movement (kinetic energy) to improve one's self.

The philosophy of energy in Islam gives us a broad perspective of life from the standpoint of consciousness and metaphysics. The interaction between our conscious mind and self-awareness, perception, reasoning, and imagination helps us better understand how to positively energize ourselves to enhance our well-being. The concept of metaphysics enlightens us relative to the perfectly arranged and well-ordered Universe, the nature of our existence, and the quest for knowledge to displace ignorance.

Islamic history is replete with examples of how energy transformed the *Ummah* (community). The Great Prophets of Noah, Abraham, Moses, Jesus and Mohammad all possessed the Divine Energy transmitted to them by the Divine Grace of God. For example, Divine Energy was transmitted to Prophet Mohammad by (a) purification and enlightenment of his body, mind and soul; (b) awareness and self-realization of God; (c) revelation of the Qur'an; (d) ascent (*mi'raj*) following a sequence of experiences; (e) manifestation of his purpose and resolve; (f) vision of spiritual and cultural transformation of the society; (g) establishment of a system of ethics, virtues and justice; and (h) transfer of power and divine leadership to the Imamat. Imam Ali Ibn Abi Talib and the Imamat that follow portray yet another example of this Divine Energy. I demonstrated how, in the history of Islam, energy was transmitted from one person to another during the tragic event of Karbala, for example, the triad of Imam Hussein, Lady Zainab, and Imam Ali Zein al-Abideen.

The quality of our lives can improve or diminish depending on how energy flows through our human system. In order to prosper in our lives, we need positive energy. We should follow the examples of our Prophets and Imams who had a positive attitude and positive behavior in life, which attracted positive energy. The example of Imam Ja'far as-Sadiq is truly inspiring, as his gift to mankind in the field of electromagnetic energy has enlightened scholars, philosophers, scientists, and physicians. We must harness our positive energy to replace fatigue with physical and emotional vigor. Pursuing a spiritual path and learning to appreciate the blessings that God has given us helps our energy fields become more focused and directed. Unquestionably, there is a direct connection between energy and the way we live. Let us make the best of the energy that God has given us.

BIBLIOGRAPHY

Abi Taleb, Imam Ali Ibn. *Nahjul Balagah.* (Translated by Farouk Ebeid). Beirut, Lebanon: Dar Al-Kitab Al-Lubnani, First Edition, 1989.

Adler, Richard B., Lan Jen Chu, and Robert M. Fano. *Electromagnetic Energy Transmission and Radiation.* Cambridge: The MIT Press, 1968.

Alakbarli, Farid. *A 13th-Century Darwin? Tusi's View on Evolution.* Azerbaijan International, Summer 2001.

Al-Farabi, Abu Nasr Muhammad (872 AD – 950 AD). *Risala Fi'l-'Aql (Epistle on the Intellect),* ed. M. Bouyges. Beirut: Imprimerie Catholique, 1938, p. 120.

Al-Ghazali, Abu Hamid Muhammad ibn Muhammad (1058 AD – 1111 AD). *Ihya' 'Ulum al-Din (The Revival of the Religious Sciences.* Cairo: Matba'ah Lajnah Nashr al-Thaqafah al-Islamiyyah, 1937-1938, 5 vols.

Ali, Abdullah Yusuf. *The Holy Qur'an: Text, Translation and Commentary.* Washington, D.C.: The Islamic Center, 1978.

Ali, S. V. Mir Ahmed. *Husain: The Saviour of Islam.* Qum, Iran: Ansariyan Publications, Second Edition, 2005.

Ali, S. V. Mir Ahmed. *The Holy Qur'an.* Elmhurst, New York: Tahrike Tarsile Qur'an, Inc., 1995.

Al-Jawziyya (1292 AD – 1350 AD). *Natural Healing With the Medicine of the Prophet; Translated and Emended by al-Akil, M.* Pearl Publishing House, 1993.

Al Kashani, Mullah Faidh. *Me'raj – The Night Ascension.* (Translated by Saleem Bhimji). Canada: Islamic Humanitarian Service, 1997.

Alkassimi, Sherif. *The Qur'an on the Expanding Universe and the Big Bang Theory.* IslamReligion.com, July 1, 2008.

Al-Majlisi, Muhammad Baqir. *Bihar al-Anwar (Ocean of Light).* Encyclopedia of Hadiths, 17th Century.

Al- Mufid, Shaykh. *Kitab Al-Irshad: The Book of Guidance into the Lives of the Twelve Imams.* (Translated by I. K. A. Howard). Tehran: Ansariyan Publication, (no date).

Al-Qarashi, Baqir Sharif. *The Life of Imam Husain ('a)*. (Translated by Sayyid Athar Husain S. H. Rizvi). Qum, Iran: Ansariyan Publications, First Edition, 2007.

An Analysis of the Characteristics of Imam Hussein. World Service of Islamic Republic of Iran Broadcasting Website, 2000.

Ashraf, Professor Faheem. *Islamic Concept of Creation of Universe, Big Bang and Science-Religion Interaction*. Science-Religion Dialogue, Mansehra, Pakistan: Hazara Society for Science Religion Dialogue, Spring 2003.

As-Sajjad, Imam Al'i Ibnul-Husayn Zaynul-Aa-bideen. *Al-Sahifah Al-Sajjadiyyah Al-Kamilah (The Psalms of Islam)*. (Translated by William C. Chittick). Qum: Iran, Ansariyan Publications, Fourth Edition, 2006.

Athar, Dr, Shahid Athar. *Medical Aspects of Fasting*. Islamic Horizon, May 1984.

Atkins, Peter. *Four Laws That Drive the Universe*. Oxford: Oxford University Press, 2007.

Avicenna (Ibn Sina) (980 AD – 1037 AD). *Kitab al-Shifa (The Book of Healing)*, Avicennae De Congelatione et Conglutinatione Lapidum, edited by E. J. Holmyard and D. C. Mandeville. Paris: Librairie Orientalists Paul Geunther, 1927.

Backster, C. *Evidence of a Primary Perception in Plant Life*. International Journal of Parapsychology, Volume 10, No. 4, 1968.

Bacon, T. *The Man Who Reads Nature's Secret Signals*. National Wildlife, February-March, 1969.

Behishti, Dr. M. Husayni and Dr. M. Jawad Bahonar. *Philosophy of Islam*. Jamaica, New York: Imam Al-Khoei Islamic Center.

Big Bang Theory Busted by 33 Top Scientists. New Scientist, May 22-28, 2004, p. 20.

Blank, M. *Electrical Field – Biological Interactions and Mechanisms*. Washington, D.C.: Advances in Chemistry Series 250, American Chemical Society, 1995.

Bloomfield, Maurice. *Hymns of the Atharva-Veda*. Oxford: At The Clarendon Press, 1897.

Brennan, B. *Hands of Healing: A Guide to Healing Through the Human Energy Field*. New York: Bantam Books, 1987.

Bullock, C. Hassell. *An Introduction to the Old Testament Prophetic Books*. Chicago: Moody Publishers, Revised Edition, 2007.

Carbon in the Air. realcarboncreditsnow.com, 2008.

Carroll, Will. *The Health Benefits of Fasting.* Bryn Mawr, Pennsylvania: Bryn Mawr College, 2002.

Cornish-Bowden, Athel and Maria Luz Cardenas. *Control of Metabolic Processes.* New York: Plenum Publishing Corporation, 1990.

Craig, William Lane. *The Kalam Cosmological Argument.* Eugene, Oregon: Wipf & Stock Publishers, 2000.

Dennison, Paul and Gail Dennison. *Brain Gym ® Teacher's Edition Revisited.* Ventura, California: Edu-Kinesthetics, Inc., 1994, p. 40.

Denton, Michael J. *Nature's Destiny.* The Free Press, 1998.

DePinna, Simon. *Transfer of Energy (Gareth Stevens Vital Science: Physical Science).* Grand Haven, Michigan: Gareth Stevens Publishing, 2007.

Dincer, Ibrahim and Marc A. Rosen. *Thermal Energy Storage: Systems and Applications.* Hoboken, New Jersey: Wiley, 2002.

Dobrin, R., B. Conaway and J. Pierrakos. *Instrumental Measurements of the Human Energy Field.* New York: Institute of the New Age, 1978.

Fife, Bruce Fife. *The Detox Book: How to Detoxify Your Body to Improve Your Health, Stop Disease, and Reverse Aging.* Colorado Springs, Colorado: Picadilly Books, Ltd., Second Edition, 2001.

Forlaget Illuminated Sweden. *Bible Illuminated: The Book New Testament.* Stockholm: Illuminated World, 2008.

Frank-Kamenetskii, D. A. *Plasma, the Fourth State of Matter.* New York: Plenum Press, 1972.

Freeman, Ken and Geoff McNamara. *In Search of Dark Matter.* New York: Springer, First Edition, 2006.

Frisch, Priscilla Frisch. *The Galactic Environment of the Sun.* American Scientist, January-February 2000.

Garrett, E. *Awareness.* New York: Berkeley Publishing Corporation, 1968.

George Smoot Wins Nobel Prize in Physics. University of California at Berkeley, 2006 Nobel Prize in Physics, October 2006.

Ghazzawi, Dr. Zaid. *The Law of Everything as Derived from the Noble Qur'an.* Amman, Jordan: Hashemite University, First Edition, 2004.

Goldstein, Jack. *Triumph Over Disease by Fasting and Natural Diet.* New York: Arco Publishing Company, Inc., 1977.

Goleman, Dr. Daniel. *Emotional Intelligence.* New York: Bantam Books, 1995.

Hackett, Stuart C. *The Resurrection of Theism: Prolegomena to Christian Apology.* Chicago: Moody Press, 1957.

Hadley, Debbie. *How Do Bees Make Honey?* 2009 About.com, The New York Times Company.

Haeri, Shaykh Fadhlalla. *The Origin of Islam and Its Universal Truth.* Internet.

Hornecker, John. *Cosmic Insights into Human Consciousness.* Internet, 1996.

Hosein, Imran N. *The Scientific Significance of Isra' and Miraj: Article 5, Various Dimensions of Miraj.* New Jersey: Al-Huda Foundation.

Howard, Dr. I.K.A. *Al-Kafi by Al-Kulayni.* Al-Serat, Volume 2, No. 1, 1976.

Huse, S. M. *The Collapse of Evolution.* Grand Rapids, Michigan: Baker Books, 1983.

Ibn Miskawayh, Ahmad Ibn Muhammad Ibn Ya'qub (932 AD – 1030 AD). *Tahdhib al-Akhlaq*, English translation by Constantine K. Zurayk. Beirut: American University of Beirut, 1968.

Ibrahim, I. A. *A Brief Illustrated Guide to Understanding Islam.* Houston: Darussalam Publishers and Distributors, Second Edition, 1997.

Inati, Shams C. *Epistemology in Islamic Philosophy.* Routledge, 1998.

Islamic Foundation for Ecology and Environmental Sciences, London, United Kingdom. *Glossary of Environment Statistics, Studies in Methods, Series F, No. 67.* New York: United Nations, 1997.

Isles, Greg. *Dark Matter.* Philadelphia: Coronet, 2004.

Ivry, Alfred L. *Al-Kindi's Metaphysics: A Translation of the Treatise on First Philosophy.* New York: State University of New York Press, 1974.

Jafery, Syed Mohammed Askari. *Nahjul Balagah: Sermons, letters and saying of Hazrat Ali.* New York: Tahrike Tarsile Qur'an, 1981.

Kabbani, Shaykh Hisham Muhammad. *Spiritual Healing in the Islamic Tradition.* Boston: Harvard Medical School's Spirituality & Healing in Medicine – II, 1997.

Katz, Heidi. *Managing Energy for Sustained High Performance.* Senior Consultant, PROACTION, 2006.

Kermalli, Jameel. *Islam the Absolute Truth: A Comprehensive Approach to Understanding Islam's Beliefs and Practices.* Sanford, Florida: Zahra Foundation, First Edition, 2008.

Khan, Hafiz Owais-Ur-Rehman. *Scientific Explanation for the Event of Miraj.* April 22, 2008.

Khan, Muhammad Muhsin. *The Translation of the Meanings of Sahih Al-Bukhari: Arabic-English.* Riyadh, Saudi Arabia: Maktabat Al-Riyadh Al-Hadeethah, Vols. 1-9, 1982.

Kilner, W. *The Human Aura.* New York: University Books, 1965.

Kustes, Scott. *Part 1: What Happens to Your Body When You Fast? – Energy Production.* ModernForager.com, 2008.

Lama, Dalai. *The Dalai Lama's Book of Wisdom.* London: Thorsons Publishers, 2000.

Lari, Sayyid Mujtaba Musavi. *Imamate and Leadership: Lessons on Islamic Doctrine (Book Four)* (Translated by Hamid Algar). Tehran: Iran, Foundation of Islamic Cultural Propagation in the World, First Edition, 1996.

Lights and Disease. The Minister, 11:10, p. 5-7, 1984.

Loehr, Jim and Tony Schwartz. *Power of Full Engagement.* New York: Free Press, a Division of Simon & Schuster, Inc., 2003.

McCutcheon, Mark. *The Final Theory: Rethinking Our Scientific Legacy.* Boca Raton, Florida: Universal Publishers, Second Edition, 2004.

Meteorites Supplied Earth Life with Phosphorous, Scientists Say. University of Arizona, 2004.

Mudulood World News. *Scientists' Comments on the Qur'an.* www.mudulood.com.

Mutahheri, Allamah Murtaza. *Man and Universe.* Pakistan: Al-Khoei Foundation, 1991.

Mutahhari, Murtada. *Polarization around the Character of 'Ali Ibn Abi Talib.* Tehran, Iran: Wofis, World Organization for Islamic Services, First Edition, 1981.

Najafi, I. H. *Ghadeer-E-Khum Where The Religion Was Brought To Perfection.* Tehran, Iran: A Group of Muslim Brothers, 1974.

Nicolson, Iain. *Dark Side of the Universe: Dark Matter, Dark Energy, and the Fate of the Cosmos.* Baltimore: The Johns Hopkins University Press, 2007.

Nowacki, Mark R. *The Kalam Cosmological Argument for God.* New York: Prometheus Books, 2007.

Oddenino, Kathy, R.N. *Bridges of Consciousness: Self Discovery in the New Age.* Joy Publications, October 1989.

Payne, B. *The Body Magnetic.* Santa Cruz, California: Fourth Edition, 1988.

Pierrakos, John C. *The Core Energetic Process.* New York: Institute of the New Age (Monograph), 1977.

Pierrakos, John C. *The Energy Field in Man and Nature.* New York: Institute of Bioenergetic Analysis, 1971.

Poling, Bruce, John M. Prausnitz, and John P. O'Connell. *The Properties of Gases and Liquids.* McGraw-Hill Education-Europe, Fifth Edition, 2000.

Poole, Judith. *More than Meets the Eye: Energy.* Massachusetts: Pooled Resources, 1999.

Prophet Muhammad's Night Journey to the Seven Heavens (peace be upon him). maniacmuslim.com, June 2, 2008.

Research Committee of Strasbourg, France (Thesis). *The Great Muslim Scientist and Philosopher – Imam Jafar Ibn Mohammed As-Sadiq (a.s.)* (Translated from the Persian book, *Maghze Mutafakkir Jehan Shia*). Ontario, Canada: Second Edition, 1997.

Russell, Walter. *The Message of the Divine Iliad (Vol. 1).* Waynesboro, Virginia: University of Science & Philosophy, 1971.

Savage, N. E. and R. S. Wood. *General Science: Matter and Energy Book 1.* New York: Routledge, Second Edition, 1979.

Schwartz, Gary E. R. and Linda G. S. Russek. *The Living Energy Universe.* Charlottesville, Virginia: Hampton Roads Publishing Company, Inc., 1999.

Shahin, Badr. *Lady Zaynab (Peace Be Upon Her).* Qum: Iran, Ansaryian Publications.

Shepherd, Peter. *Emotional Intelligence.* Trasn4mind.net website.

Swan, J. *Nature as Healer.* New York: Villiard Books, 1992.

Tabataba'i, Sayyid Muhammad Husayn. *Elements of Islamic Metaphysics (Bidayat al-Hikmah)* (Translated by Sayyid 'Ali Quli Qara'i). Palgrave Macmillan, 2003.

Tabataba'i, Sayyid Muhammad Husayn. *Shi'ite Islam* (Translated by Sayyid Husayn Nasr). State University of New York Press, Second Edition, 1979.

Terrific Science Press and National Science Foundation. *Exploring Energy with TOYS: Mechanical Energy and Energy Conversions (Teaching Science with TOYS)*. Blue Ridge Summit, Pennsylvania, TAB Books, Inc., 1997.

The Concept of Life in Islam. IslamOnline.net, 2002.

The Equivalence of Mass and Energy. Stanford Encyclopedia of Philosophy, 2007.

The Number 19. VirtueScience.com.

Tomecek, Steve. *Dirtmeister's Science Lab on Matter: What Is Matter? How Does It Change Forms?* New York: Scholastic.

Turfe, Tallal Alie. *Unity in Islam: Reflections and Insights*. Elmhurst, New York: Tahrike Tarsile Qur'an, Inc., 2004.

Turfe, Tallal Alie. *Patience in Islam: Sabr*. Elmhurst, New York: Tahrike Tarsile Qur'an, Inc., 1996.

United Nations Environment Programme (UNEP). Nairobi, Kenya.

Van der Zwaan, B. C. C., C. R. Hill, A. L. Mechelynck, and G. Ripka. *Nuclear Energy: Promise or Peril?* Singapore: World Scientific Publishing Company, 1999.

Watson, David. *The Conservation of Energy and the First Law of Thermodynamics*. FT Exploring, david.flyingturtle@gmail.com, 2005.

Whitney, Rich and Livia M. D'Andrea. *The Process of Becoming a Leader: An Individual Identity Model*. Alexandria, Virginia: American Counseling Association, Vistas 2007.

Wikipedia Encyclopedia.

Williams, George. *Relationship of Matter and Energy and the Application to the First Cause*. Internet.

Yahya, Harun. *The Miracle of the Honeybee*. 2009 by Harun Yahya International.

FOOTNOTES

[1] Iain Nicolson, *Dark Side of the Universe: Dark Matter, Dark Energy, and the Fate of the Cosmos* (Baltimore: The Johns Hopkins University Press, 2007).

[2] Ken Freeman and Geoff McNamara, *In Search of Dark Matter* (New York: Springer, First Edition, 2006).

[3] Bruce E. Poling, John M. Prausnitz, and John P. O'Connell, *The Properties of Gases and Liquids* (McGraw-Hill Education-Europe, Fifth Edition, 2000).

[4] Ibid.

[5] Ibid.

[6] D. A. Frank-Kamenetskii, *Plasma, the Fourth State of Matter* (New York: Plenum Press, 1972).

[7] George Williams, *Relationship of Matter and Energy and the Application to the First Cause* (Internet).

[8] Steve Tomecek, *Dirtmeister's Science Lab on Matter: What Is Matter? How Does It Change Forms?* (New York: Scholastic).

[9] *The Equivalence of Mass and Energy* (Stanford Encyclopedia of Philosophy, 2007).

[10] Peter Atkins, *Four Laws That Drive the Universe* (Oxford: Oxford University Press, 2007).

[11] Farid Alakbarli, A 13th-Century Darwin? Tusi's View on Evolution (Azerbaijan International, Summer 2001).

[12] Ibid.

[13] *Big Bang Theory Busted by 33 Top Scientists* (New Scientist, May 22-28, 2004, p. 20).

[14] *George Smoot Wins Nobel Prize in Physics* (University of California at Berkeley, 2006 Nobel Prize in Physics, October 2006).

[15] Sherif Alkassimi, *The Qur'an on the Expanding Universe and the Big Bang Theory* (IslamReligion.com, July 1, 2008).

[16] Professor Faheem Ashraf, *Islamic Concept of Creation of Universe, Big Bang and Science-Religion Interaction* (Science-Religion Dialogue, Mansehra, Pakistan: Hazara Society for Science Religion Dialogue, Spring 2003).

[17] Imam Ali Ibn Abi Taleb, *Nahjul Balagah* (Translated by Farouk Ebeid) (Beirut, Lebanon: Dar Al-Kitab Al-Lubnani, First Edition, 1989).

[18] Alfred L. Ivry, *Al-Kindi's Metaphysics: A Translation of the Treatise on First Philosophy* (New York: State University of New York Press, 1974).

[19] Ibid.

[20] Ibid.

[21] Stuart C. Hackett, *The Resurrection of Theism: Prolegomena to Christian Apology* (Chicago: Moody Press, 1957).

[22] William Lane Craig, *The Kalam Cosmological Argument* (Eugene, Oregon: Wipf & Stock Publishers, 2000).

[23] Mark R. Nowacki, *The Kalam Cosmological Argument for God* (New York: Prometheus Books, 2007).

[24] Dr. M. Husayni Behishti and Dr. M. Jawad Bahonar, *Philosophy of Islam* (Jamaica, New York: Imam Al-Khoei Islamic Center).

[25] *Carbon in the Air* (realcarboncreditsnow.com, 2008).

[26] Simon DePinna, *Transfer of Energy (Gareth Stevens Vital Science: Physical Science)* (Grand Haven, Michigan: Gareth Stevens Publishing, 2007).

[27] Ibid.

[28] Avicenna (Ibn Sina) (980 AD – 1037 AD), *Kitab al-Shifa (The Book of Healing)*, Avicennae De Congelatione et Conglutinatione Lapidum, edited by E. J. Holmyard and D. C. Mandeville (Paris: Librairie Orientalists Paul Geunther, 1927).

[29] Ibrahim Dincer and Marc A. Rosen, *Thermal Energy Storage: Systems and Applications* (Hoboken, New Jersey: Wiley, 2002).

[30] N. E. Savage and R. S. Wood, *General Science: Matter and Energy Book 1* (New York: Routledge, Second Edition, 1979).

[1] B. C. C. van der Zwaan, C. R. Hill, A. L. Mechelynck, and G. Ripka, *Nuclear Energy: Promise or Peril?* (Singapore: World Scientific Publishing Company, 1999).

[2] Terrific Science Press and National Science Foundation, *Exploring Energy with TOYS: Mechanical Energy and Energy Conversions (Teaching Science with TOYS)* (Blue Ridge Summit, Pennsylvania, TAB Books, Inc., 1997).

[3] Richard B. Adler, Lan Jen Chu, and Robert M. Fano, *Electromagnetic Energy Transmission and Radiation* (Cambridge: The MIT Press, 1968).

[4] Athel Cornish-Bowden and Maria Luz Cardenas, *Control of Metabolic Processes* (New York: Plenum Publishing Corporation, 1990).

[5] David Watson, *The Conservation of Energy and the First Law of Thermodynamics* (FT Exploring, david.flyingturtle@gmail.com, 2005).

[6] S. M. Huse, *The Collapse of Evolution* (Grand Rapids, Michigan: Baker Books, 1983).

[7] John Hornecker, *Cosmic Insights into Human Consciousness* (Internet, 1996).

[8] Paul Dennison and Gail Dennison, *Brain Gym ® Teacher's Edition Revisited* (Ventura, California: Edu-Kinesthetics, Inc., 1994, p. 40).

[9] Abu Hamid Muhammad ibn Muhammad Al-Ghazali (1058 AD – 1111 AD), *Ihya' 'Ulum al-Din (The Revival of the Religious Sciences)* (Cairo: Matba'ah Lajnah Nashr al-Thaqafah al-Islamiyyah, 1937-1938, 5 vols.).

[10] Dr. I.K.A. Howard, *Al-Kafi by Al-Kulayni* (Al-Serat, Volume 2, No. 1, 1976).

[11] Scott Kustes, *Part 1: What Happens to Your Body When You Fast? – Energy Production* (ModernForager.com, 2008).

[12] Dr, Shahid Athar, *Medical Aspects of Fasting* (Islamic Horizon, May 1984).

[13] Bruce Fife, *The Detox Book: How to Detoxify Your Body to Improve Your Health, Stop Disease, and Reverse Aging* (Colorado Springs, Colorado: Picadilly Books, Ltd., Second Edition, 2001).

[14] Jack Goldstein, *Triumph Over Disease by Fasting and Natural Diet* (New York: Arco Publishing Company, Inc., 1977).

[15] Will Carroll, *The Health Benefits of Fasting* (Bryn Mawr, Pennsylvania: Bryn Mawr College, 2002).

[46] Dr. Daniel Goleman, *Emotional Intelligence* (New York: Bantam Books, 1995).

[47] Peter Shepherd, *Emotional Intelligence* (Trasn4mind.net website).

[48] Walter Russell, *The Message of the Divine Iliad* (Vol. 1) (Waynesboro, Virginia: University of Science & Philosophy, 1971).

[49] Shaykh Hisham Muhammad Kabbani, MD, *Spiritual Healing in the Islamic Tradition* (Boston: Harvard Medical School's Spirituality & Healing in Medicine – II, 1997).

[50] Dr. Zaid Ghazzawi, *The Law of Everything as Derived from the Noble Qur'an* (Amman, Jordan: Hashemite University, First Edition, 2004).

[51] Jim Loehr and Tony Schwartz, *Power of Full Engagement* (New York: Free Press, a Division of Simon & Schuster, Inc., 2003).

[52] Heidi Katz, *Managing Energy for Sustained High Performance* (Senior Consultant, PROACTION, 2006).

[53] C. Hassell Bullock, *An Introduction to the Old Testament Prophetic Books* (Chicago: Moody Publishers, Revised Edition, 2007).

[54] Forlaget Illuminated Sweden, *Bible Illuminated: The Book New Testament* (Stockholm: Illuminated World, 2008).

[55] Dalai Lama, *The Dalai Lama's Book of Wisdom* (London: Thorsons Publishers, 2000).

[56] Maurice Bloomfield, *Hymns of the Atharva-Veda* (Oxford: At The Clarendon Press, 1897).

[57] United Nations Environment Programme (UNEP), Nairobi, Kenya.

[58] Islamic Foundation for Ecology and Environmental Sciences (London, United Kingdom).

[59] *Glossary of Environment Statistics, Studies in Methods, Series F, No. 67* (New York: United Nations, 1997).

[60] Jameel Kermalli, *Islam the Absolute Truth: A Comprehensive Approach to Understanding Islam's Beliefs and Practices* (Sanford, Florida: Zahra Foundation, First Edition, 2008).

[61] Syed Mohammed Askari Jafery, *Nahjul Balagah: Sermons, letters and saying of Hazrat Ali* (New York: Tahrike Tarsile Qur'an, 1981).

[62] Abu Hamid Muhammad ibn Muhammad Al-Ghazali (1058 AD – 1111 AD), *Ihya' 'Ulum al-Din (The Revival of the Religious Sciences)* (Cairo: Matba'ah Lajnah Nashr al-Thaqafah al-Islamiyyah, 1937-1938, 5 vols.).

[63] Mudulood World News, *Scientists' Comments on the Qur'an* (www.mudulood.com).

[64] *Meteorites Supplied Earth Life with Phosphorous, Scientists Say* (University of Arizona, 2004).

[65] Priscilla Frisch, *The Galactic Environment of the Sun* (American Scientist, January-February 2000).

[66] Michael J. Denton, *Nature's Destiny* (The Free Press, 1998).

[67] I. A. Ibrahim, *A Brief Illustrated Guide to Understanding Islam* (Houston: Darussalam Publishers and Distributors, Second Edition, 1997).

[68] *The Number 19* (VirtueScience.com).

[69] Debbie Hadley, *How Do Bees Make Honey?* (2009 About.com, The New York Times Company).

[70] Harun Yahya, *The Miracle of the Honeybee* (2009 by Harun Yahya International).

[71] Shaykh Fadhlalla Haeri, *The Origin of Islam and Its Universal Truth* (Internet).

[72] Jameel Kermalli, *Islam the Absolute Truth: A Comprehensive Approach to Understanding Islam's Beliefs and Practices* (Sanford, Florida: Zahra Foundation, First Edition, 2008).

[73] Wikipedia Encyclopedia.

[74] Imam Ali Ibn Abi Taleb, *Nahjul Balagah* (Translated by Farouk Ebeid) (Beirut: Lebanon, Dar Al-Kitab Al-Lubnani, First Edition, 1989).

[75] Sayyid Muhammad Husayn Tabataba'i, *Shi'ite Islam* (Translated by Sayyid Husayn Nasr) (State University of New York Press, Second Edition, 1979).

[76] Sayyid Muhammad Husayn Tabataba'i, *Elements of Islamic Metaphysics (Bidayat al-Hikmah)* (Translated by Sayyid Ali Quli Qara'i) (Palgrave Macmillan, 2003).

[77] Kathy Oddenino, R.N., *Bridges of Consciousness: Self Discovery in the New Age* (Joy Publications, October 1989).

[78] *The Concept of Life in Islam* (IslamOnline.net, 2002).

[79] Shams C. Inati, *Epistemology in Islamic Philosophy* (Routledge, 1998).

[80] Abu Nasr Muhammad Al-Farabi (872 AD – 950 AD), *Risala Fi'l-'Aql (Epistle on the Intellect)*, ed. M. Bouyges (Beirut: Imprimerie Catholique, 1938, p. 120).

[81] Ibid.

[82] Ahmad Ibn Muhammad Ibn Ya'qub Ibn Miskawayh (932 AD – 1030 AD), *Tahdhib al-Akhlaq*, English translation by Constantine K. Zurayk (Beirut: American University of Beirut, 1968).

[83] Mullah Faidh Al Kashani, *Me'raj – The Night Ascension* (Translated by Saleem Bhimji) (Canada: Islamic Humanitarian Service, 1997).

[84] Hafiz Owais-Ur-Rehman Khan, *Scientific Explanation for the Event of Miraj* (April 22, 2008).

[85] *Prophet Muhammad's Night Journey to the Seven Heavens (peace be upon him)* (maniacmuslim.com, June 2, 2008).

[86] Imran N. Hosein, *The Scientific Significance of Isra' and Miraj: Article 5, Various Dimensions of Miraj* (New Jersey: Al-Huda Foundation).

[87] I. H. Najafi, *Ghadeer-E-Khum Where the Religion Was Brought To Perfection* (Tehran, Iran: A Group of Muslim Brothers, 1974).

[88] Murtada Mutahhari, *Polarization around the Character of 'Ali Ibn Abi Talib* (Tehran, Iran: Wofis, World Organization for Islamic Services, First Edition, 1981).

[89] Sayyid Mujtaba Musavi Lari, *Imamate and Leadership: Lessons on Islamic Doctrine (Book Four)* (Translated by Hamid Algar) (Tehran: Foundation of Islamic Cultural Propagation in the World, First Edition, 1996).

[90] Shaykh Al- Mufid, *Kitab Al-Irshad: The Book of Guidance into the Lives of the Twelve Imams* (Translated by I. K. A. Howard) (Tehran: Ansariyan Publication, no date).

[91] Baqir Sharif al-Qarashi, *The Life of Imam Husain ('a)* (Translated by Sayyid Athar Husain S. H. Rizvi) (Qum, Iran: Ansariyan Publications, First Edition, 2007).

[92] *An Analysis of the Characteristics of Imam* Hussein (World Service of Islamic Republic of Iran Broadcasting Website, 2000).

[93] Badr Shahin, *Lady Zaynab (Peace Be Upon Her)* (Qum: Iran, Ansaryian Publications).

[94] Rich Whitney and Livia M. D'Andrea, *The Process of Becoming a Leader: An Individual Identity Model* (Alexandria, Virginia, American Counseling Association, Vistas 2007).

[95] Imam Al'i Ibnul-Husayn Zaynul-Aa'bideen as-Sajjad, *Al-Sahifah Al-Sajjadiyyah Al-Kamilah (The Psalms of Islam)* (Translated by William C. Chittick) (Qum: Iran, Ansariyan Publications, Fourth Edition, 2006).

[96] Research Committee of Strasbourg, France (Thesis), *The Great Muslim Scientist and Philosopher – Imam Jafar Ibn Mohammed As-Sadiq (a.s.)* (Translated from the Persian book, Maghze Mutafakkir Jehan Shia) (Ontario, Canada: Kaukab Ali Mirza Publisher, Second Edition, 1997).

[97] Ibid.

[98] Ibid.

[99] Ibid.

[100] Ibid.

[101] Ibid.

[102] Ibid.

[103] Ibid.

[104] Ibid.

[105] *Lights and Disease* (The Minister, 11:10, p. 5-7, 1984).

[106] Wikipedia Encyclopedia.